NAVIGATING YOUR
change mazes

NAVIGATING YOUR
change mazes

INCREASE YOUR RELIANCE ON GOD AS YOUR GUIDE

TOM LUTZ

Evergreen
Press

© Copyright 2006, Lutz Group International®

First Published in the United States by:
Evergreen Press of Brainerd, LLC.
201 West Laurel Street
P.O. Box 465
Brainerd, MN 56401
(218) 828-6424
www.evergreenpress.net

All rights reserved. No part of this work covered by copyrights here on may be reproduced or used in any form or by any means—graphics, electronic, or mechanical; including photocopying, scanning, taping of information on storage and retrieval systems—without prior written permission of the author, Tom Lutz.

Scripture references have been taken from the
NEW AMERICAN STANDARD BIBLE®,
Copyright ©1960, 1962, 1963, 1971, 1972, 1973, 1975, 1977, 1995
by The Lockman Foundation. Used by permission.

Concept and Text: **Tom Lutz**

Project Manager: **Chip Borkenhagen**

Editor: **Tracey Finck**

Copy Editor: **Jodi Schwen**

Design/Production: **Brad Raymond**

ISBN 0-9755252-2-0
Printed in the United States of America

In memory of our son, Timothy Paul,
and my dad, Thomas Daniel

NAVIGATING YOUR
change mazes

1	PREFACE
3	INTRODUCTION
7	SECTION 1 **Change 101: Change Maze Perspectives**
9	CHAPTER 1 Kinds of Change Mazes and Characteristics that Shape Them
23	CHAPTER 2 Change Dimensions and Changer Types
42	CHAPTERS 1 & 2 PonderPoints
45	SECTION 2 **Your Personal Navigation Kit: A Way of Life**
47	CHAPTER 3 Navigating Changes You Know Are Coming
52	CHAPTER 3 PonderPoints
55	CHAPTER 4 Understanding the Birth/Growing/Aging/Death Life-Cycle
64	CHAPTER 4 PonderPoints
65	CHAPTER 5 Planning Changes: Blending the Predictable with Your Agendas
77	CHAPTER 5 PonderPoints
79	CHAPTER 6 Navigating Unpredictable Changes: Sporadic and Blind-Side
87	CHAPTER 6 PonderPoints
89	CHAPTER 7 Managing the Trauma of Blind-Side Changes: Hitting the Wall
102	CHAPTER 7 PonderPoints
105	CHAPTER 8 Reducing the Impact when Walls Are Inevitable
114	CHAPTER 8 PonderPoints

Contents

117 SECTION 3: **Using the Spiritual Dimension to Navigate Better**

119 CHAPTER 9 **The Ultimate Change: Becoming a Christ-follower**

125 CHAPTER 9 **PonderPoints**

129 CHAPTER 10 **The Resulting Change: From Self-Centered to Christ-Centered**

139 CHAPTER 10 **PonderPoints**

141 CHAPTER 11 **Now You're Equipped to Decide: To Change or Not to Change**

151 CHAPTER 11 **PonderPoints**

153 SECTION 4 **Emerging from the Maze**

155 CHAPTER 12 **What Does It Mean to Navigate Successfully?**

165 CHAPTER 13 **The Spiritual Perspective**

172 CHAPTERS 12 & 13 **PonderPoints**

175 SECTION 5 **What if You're Called to Lead Change?**

177 CHAPTER 14 **Making Change**

187 CHAPTER 15 **Role of a Difference Maker**

195 CHAPTER 14 & 15 **PonderPoints**

199 SUMMARY & CONCLUSIONS

228 ACKNOWLEDGEMENTS

230 FOLLOW-UP WITH TOM LUTZ

Preface

Years ago, while traveling north of London, I had an opportunity to try to find my way through a famous maze that was designed and built in the eighteenth century. It was made of hedges about ten feet high with paths four feet wide, and it covered about two acres of land. The entrance was clearly marked, and the challenge was simply to emerge at the exit on the far side. When I looked into the entrance, I could see a hedge wall and the immediate necessity of choosing to turn left or right. Some people would look in that entrance and refuse to enter. Others would move forward, carefully trying to remember how to back out. And then there were those who believed it to be easy; they would walk right in.

Would you believe it took me more than an hour to navigate through the maze and find my way out? Once I had made a few turns and encountered dead ends of 10-foot high hedges, I was completely confused and certainly lost. And all I was doing was walking around a two-acre piece of land! But it certainly was confusing. I started out being really cool about the whole thing, and then uneasiness set in as I moved through a few corridors. Had I made this turn before? Was this a familiar place or was this somewhere new? Could I back out? Where was the trail of breadcrumbs that I should have left along the way? I began to walk more quickly. The dead ends were so short that I couldn't really run, but I wanted to. Could I climb the hedge and see over the top? No, it was just too high. Was I closer to the perimeter of the maze or was I getting in deeper? Was it going to get dark before I found the exit? Would I ever find my way out? If only I had a diagram of the maze, then I could have followed it like a map. But I had no map and no navigational clues. I felt *trapped*.

Finding our way through changes is often like trying to successfully find our way through a maze. The outcome of change in our lives is often unknown at the time the change hits us. Naturally, we're apprehensive. We have questions such as: *Where is this change going to lead me? How does this change impact my plans? What is this change going to do to my future? Where do I turn next to avoid getting hurt by this change? Can I go back to where I was before this change ever came along?*

Over the years as I have worked with people who are confronted with change, I have come to realize that we are all like people standing at the threshold of a maze. No matter whether we enter by choice or we get shoved, we are quickly faced with the need to decide which turn to take. And even with the best planning, we don't really know what the results might be or how long we'll be stuck in the change maze.

If only we had a map and Global Positioning System (GPS). Or better yet, someone looking down on the maze, aware of where we are, and willing to guide us on a successful trip through the change maze. Even if that maze is terribly difficult and complex and full of uncertainty and dead-ends with high walls, just knowing that someone is watching, caring, and guiding would go a long way toward taking the panic, frustration, and fear out of the change.

The intent of this book is to change the way you think about change. It should lead you to developing your own approaches and tools to help you find your way through the many change mazes you encounter along the journey of your life. But most of all, it is intended to help you gain confidence and faith in a loving God who is able to use change mazes to increase your reliance on and faith in Him no matter how difficult the change may be.

Introduction

Has anyone ever asked you to name three or four people who made a profound impact on your life? If you think about it for a moment, it may have been a teacher, or a grandparent, or a pastor, or a friend. Someone who has been a truly positive influence. Or it might have been an individual you don't ever want to see again because of the negative memories, but that person seriously shaped who you are now.

I can name more than a few of those people. But I realized years ago that in addition to people, my *experiences* have significantly molded and shaped me, too. Although I've had 18-plus years of formal education, I have actually learned more from life experiences than from books and professors. And I learned more from getting it wrong the first time than I did from getting it right. Do you remember getting the wrong answer on a test and having to get it right before you could pass the course? I can still remember facts and theorems from mathematics which I didn't answer correctly and which the teacher made me do over better than the ones I got right the first time. And that was several decades ago.

Being an *experiential learner* has inspired me to use experiences to help others learn and grow. When I give lectures or lead seminars, I find that people gravitate to real-life illustrations. Many of my presentations begin with, "Let me tell you what happened to me yesterday." Not because those experiences are unique, but just the opposite; they are common to all of us. People can easily identify with the lessons, laughs, tears, mistakes, *don't-go-theres*, losses, gains, wins, griefs, and even close escapes.

If there was a bibliography for this book, you would find it to be *very* short and centered on one book, God's Word. Instead these pages are filled with RealityCases that combine personal experiences and observations to reinforce the principles and approaches discussed. (Please Note: Many of the names, places, and specific facts have been changed to honor people's privacy.). The Scriptures are used to add God's perspective and transform *head knowledge* to *heart wisdom.*

Of all the experiences that God, the Potter, has used to shape me, the ones that stand out most are *change* experiences.

For the last 20-plus years, my business has been to *consult*, mentor, and coach. I work with business executives, church leaders, politicians, school administrators, young people, married adults, seniors, haves, have-nots, and others across the ethnic spectrum in the United States and foreign countries. My fundamental approach is to help people *face* change rather than *fear* new directions as they grow and develop. The fact that I'm actually writing this book is a result of being pressured by those I mentor and those who have heard my lectures.

Let me highlight some of the changes in my life that God has used to move me to where I am. It started at an early age. My dad was a pastor, and for as long as I remember, we lived with the reality that God could call my parents to minister somewhere else at any time. The first move was when I was four. The last one was major in my life because it happened between my junior and senior year in high school. I had to leave the football team, the baseball team, a special girl friend, buddies, and a really good high school. And I liked the small town I lived in. Fortunately I saw, even in the middle of this, that God was leading my dad to a new ministry, so I didn't grumble much. As I look back, I see that the great senior year I had in an even better school and with more opportunities was part of God's plan to mold me as He wanted instead of as I wanted. That move created major change with great results. God gave me an unbelievably godly wife who has stayed at my side through all of the ensuing changes and is, beyond a doubt, my best friend, too.

But the die of being flexible about where I live had been cast. I sometimes began to anticipate the change of a move when it wasn't smart. After leaving college, I joined IBM. Everyone knew that IBM stood for *I've Been Moved* and that was just fine with me. So when we moved into our first home, I didn't even plant grass in the backyard or shrubs in the front. A few years later when the next move came, I found out that it hadn't been wise to depend on change quite so much. We would have gotten a lot better price when we sold the place if we'd have finished the yard.

Fast forwarding a few decades, I realized that God had moved me around and into a number of different circumstances according to His plan, not mine. By the time I was in my early 50s, he had steered us through numerous changes: changes in location, changes in opportunities with different companies, and even changes in profession. We had moved from Minnesota to New York, back to Minnesota, then to Connecticut, on to Boston, down to Waco, Texas, and then to Pittsburgh. I began writing this book while living in Georgia and it is being completed as we get ready to leave Minnesota and make our way to Arizona.

The change mazes God has built in front of me have really laid the groundwork for me, not only to coach and mentor on a professional level, but also to minister to clients and church leaders on a personal level. He has given me the opportunity to be a scientist, a business executive, a teacher, and a consultant working and ministering around the globe and across the United States.

Before you begin to think that all of these changes have been easy or fun, understand that many brought fear, struggles, tears, frustrations, anger, grief and more. It has taken God a long time to shape me into His image, and He isn't done yet. The change experience of losing a son to suicide was just about more than my wife and I and our other two children could bear. But it has prepared us to help others who are weeping over a lost or wayward child. Several years ago I was assigned to head a failing business that needed to be turned around. The long hours, the scarred lives, the investors that resisted change, the demanding board, and the deep and fervent prayer prepared me to help other business leaders find their way through the maze. It also helped them see Christ who can turn despair to hope.

There have also been landmark spiritual change experiences throughout my life: having a turkey of a boss after having the best, encountering a computer crash when my career seemed in the balance, raising three kids, sensing the love of Christ when He came into my life, sitting under the ministry of John Piper when I needed it most, being torn apart by executives who asked to learn about *emotional leadership,* but were indignant when the Lord was included, and working for a world-famous author and consultant who wanted every Christ-follower *out of the company.* Ultimately, these were all spiritual change experiences.

Through these many change experiences, God has taught me a great deal about navigating change mazes. The tools and principles examined in this book have been tested in the fire of real life and found to be useful. Men and women who have learned and applied these insights have been helped as they confront and navigate their own change mazes. Most importantly, some have come closer to the Guide who builds or allows the mazes and then helps us navigate through them.

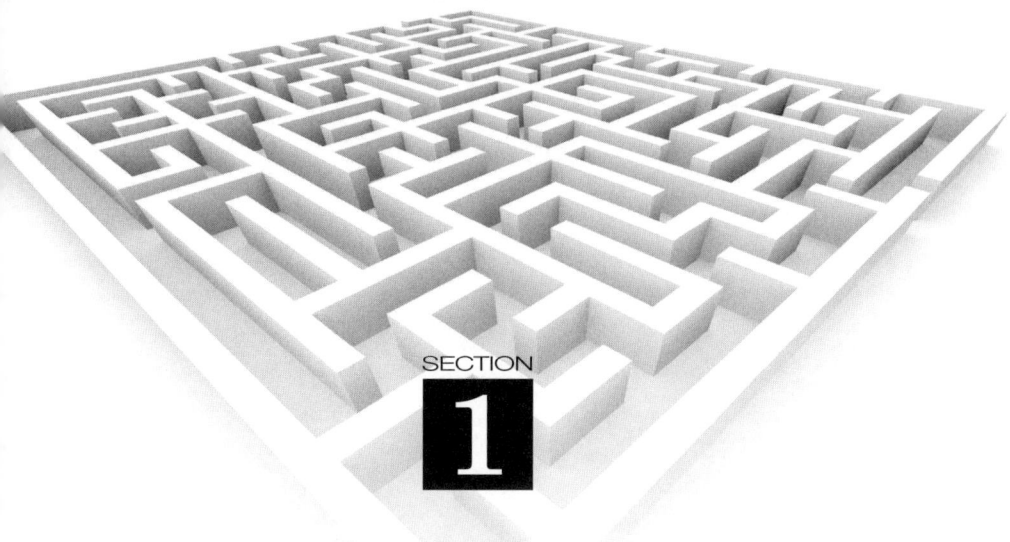

SECTION 1

CHANGE 101:
change maze perspectives

Before we get into the specifics of tools to navigate through and within change mazes, let's take a close look at both *change* and *changers*. The two chapters in this section are designed to provide an overview that equips you to understand change and, even more importantly, understand yourself as you wind your way into, within, through, and sometimes out of the maze.

This 101 section is designed to serve as the *Introduction to Change* and a *CliffsNotes* kind of summary of the more comprehensive discussions in the following sections. After reading it, you should be prepared to identify kinds of changes, understand the characteristics of change, grasp the importance of the dimensions of change, place yourself on the spectrum of change capacity, and know the impact of change shapers. This framework should give you a perspective for developing navigation tools that help you with change mazes.

CHAPTER ONE
Kinds of Change Mazes
and Characteristics that Shape Them

How do you respond to changes, especially changes that surprise you? What usually drives your response to change: the facts, your emotions, the long-range impact on you? What do you do when changes seem to overwhelm you and you don't know which way to turn?

It is this *not* knowing where to turn that makes our dealing with change so similar to trying to solve a maze. We know the entry point and we know where we want to emerge from the maze, but the tricky part is working our way through those corridors in between. Usually we are presented with a maze and given a pencil to draw a line from entry to exit.

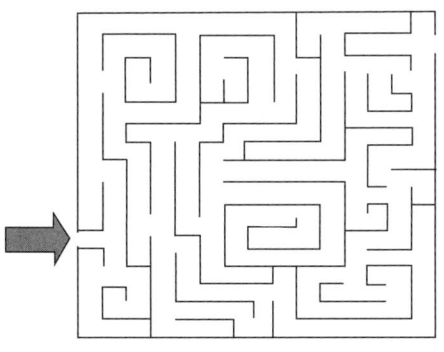

FIGURE 1.1

But let's make the decision a bit more challenging. If you don't see the whole maze because you are in it—not above it—and it is actually a labyrinth with high walls so you only see the corridor you're in and the choices to turn left, right, or go straight ahead without knowing where they lead, decisions aren't so simple. The same problem exists when you're faced with life changes. You may be able to see a few decision points ahead, but you don't really know the future or where those decisions will lead.

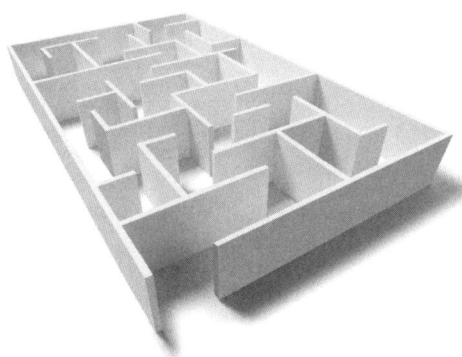

FIGURE 1.2

Consider Jeff, a friend of mine.

RealityCase

The Neighborhood Changed

The drive to get to work in normal rush hour traffic, between 6:30 and 8:30 a.m., takes over an hour when everything runs right and can be two hours when people begin to play fender bender. When Jeff bought his place in the suburbs, it took him half an hour on a good day and 55 minutes when there was trouble. The farm across the road still had cows and a beautiful red barn and tractors for the kids to watch and a rural mailbox and a dirt driveway. The closest store was two miles away and that was just fine. But three years ago, the farm was sold and a housing development with 45 houses went in. A strip mall with a dozen stores replaced the woods between him and that store two miles away. They put in a traffic light where he turns onto the state road—where the store used to be. And someone put in six traffic lights (he counted them) on the state road between that intersection and the interstate. The interstate part of his journey to the office used to be quick and easy, but now is jammed beginning at 6:30 every morning. And when it isn't moving slowly, it's a big parking lot.

Finally, between the federal government and the state legislature, two significant changes were approved—the interstate would add two more lanes going each way (it would become an eight-lane highway) and the state road would add one more lane each way. He's going to get to work in a half hour again. Oh, by the way, to get his commute changed back to the length it was when he moved to the suburbs will take three years of construction. And while that's going on, Jeff's commute will be 2 hours and 45 minutes because of the detours and temporary roadways. One other thing, on the interstate section, it will cost more to build temporary roadways to go around the construction than the actual cost of the added four lanes.

How did he get into this mess anyway? Well, the change in commute that gave Jeff heartburn was slow and subtle. Each year he lived there, the commute took 10 minutes more than the year before. Each year he figured, "I can handle it. It's just a little longer and we're so happy where we live. Now he's faced with the fact that the slow change has made the water hotter than he can stand. Remember the biology experiment—drop a frog in boiling water and it jumps right out? But if you put the frog in cool water and slowly heat the water, it stays in the pot until it's cooked (and dead).

When the kids were young and their events were held in the afternoons only, there was no way he could attend. Now they are in band concerts and games and activities that are in the evenings—and Jeff

> still can't get home from work in time to enjoy watching them. And the change required to fix it has a cost in time greater than he can face. The kids will be through high school before the new roads are in.

The initial change of moving to the suburbs was just what my friend wanted—at the time. He would get away from the hustle of where they lived before. But it is important to realize that a change you're facing may impact you very differently than what the current facts and your past experiences tell you.

As you work through this book, you'll see navigation tips that should help you find your way through change mazes. Based on the idea that you can only see a few features ahead in the maze, and experiences like my friend's, here is the first.

NAVIGATION TIP:
Be careful about assuming that you know the outcome when you only see a few potential alternatives from the maze corridor you're in.

Just as some mazes are quite simple and fun to solve, so are some of the changes we face. On the other hand there are changes that are complex and lead to results that profoundly impact our lives. Those mazes are sometimes beyond human comprehension and solution. In fact, we may enter a change maze and remain there for all or most of our lives. It is important to recognize such a maze and turn your energy toward making the change part of your life and turning it into a God-honoring process.

KINDS OF CHANGES

Here is a brief overview of the types of change mazes that will be covered in more details in later chapters.

PREDICTABLE

You have a pretty good idea of what will happen. An example of this is the life cycle of a person: birth, growth, maturing, aging, and death. For example, based on our knowledge about most kids, we know that a baby (and the whole household) will change when he moves from crawling to walking, around the age of one.

Predictable change is usually quite simple to navigate if you accept the facts and keep your emotions in check. But that isn't always easy. If you are about to turn 30 and somehow begin to resist getting older, the change can be traumatic because you have no control over the arrival of that dreaded birthday.

PLANNED

These types of changes are usually predictable because they have been planned by you or someone else and the plan is known. When you trade your older car for a newer one, you can expect your insurance premium and the license fee to increase because there are plans by the insurance company and the state to make it happen. You may not appreciate the higher costs, but you had better plan for the financial change when you consider the trade.

When you ignore the planned change, or pretend it doesn't exist, that is when you can make serious wrong turns in the change maze, even though the path through the corridors could be quite simple. If you don't update your insurance when you move to the newer automobile, and you have an accident, you'll suffer a lot of unnecessary stress.

CONTINUOUS

These changes keep on happening without interruption. Most of these types of changes are predictable, much like the life-cycle. And a continuous change maze may not have an exit. Note that there are times when the maze may just appear to go forever without a point to leave it. The limitations, the blocking of certain corridors that could provide a way of escape, might even be of your own making.

While I was teaching at Baylor University, several of my graduate students were complaining that they couldn't find employment in Waco that matched their degrees. They were faced with the change maze of taking on work that was different from what they had invested years of energy and funds to prepare for. These were bright young people with high GPAs, so it wasn't that they weren't qualified. Waco was a small city that didn't have the demand for their kind and level of profession. When I asked them if they had considered moving to other parts of Texas, or somewhere else in the United States, or even going international, they were adamant about staying in Waco. With the attitude that blocked the location-change corridor, they would remain in a continuous maze that could cause them to forego using their professional preparation.

UNPREDICTABLE

You have no idea that this type of change is coming your way. A truly unpredictable change maze that is placed in your path does not give warning. It usually catches you unprepared. Suddenly you're in the maze and wondering what happened.

Amazingly, you will seldom encounter an unpredictable change maze. Most of the time, life gives us clues. We often refuse to acknowledge the signs that a change is coming. (This is called denial.) Or we might be so preoccupied with our own agendas that we don't see the signs. Most heart attacks, for example, are predictable, but if you ignore the *predictors*, you will swear that you didn't see it coming. The tragedy of hurricane Katrina is another example. Individuals as well as local, state, and federal government all minimized the serious predictions. When the storm hit, many claimed that the severity of the storm hadn't been predicted.

SPORADIC

These are change mazes that you may suspect will occur, but the timing is unpredictable. The key here is to be prepared for sporadic changes. Your level of awareness and preparation is usually based on the impact and frequency of these changes.

Some people refuse to take out flood insurance because there hasn't been a flood that reached their doorstep (and basement) for 50 years, even though they know they're in a flood plain. And yet if such a flood occurred, it would throw them into a change maze that might cause them to expend years of effort to get out. The sporadic nature of the change lulled them into ignoring the possibility of danger. This denial of a potential destructive change has caused the United States government to insist that you obtain flood insurance if you are in a flood plain before you can get a mortgage for the purchase of your home.

BLIND-SIDE

This change maze is usually a complete and sudden surprise. You will seldom have a choice whether you will enter this kind of maze or not. It is thrust on you.

There are two components that make the blind-side change maze so difficult to navigate: (1) the change itself and (2) the way it comes into your life. If you knew it was coming, even if it was inevitable, you could usually prepare yourself for it. But when the surprise of it throws you into the middle of a very complex maze, the suddenness of the change can make you—and keep you—completely disoriented. Rational thinking becomes hard, frustration leads to more disorientation, and panic complicates the process of finding both yourself and a way to navigate the maze. In fact, this kind of change is usually overwhelming. It takes on the characteristics of being a labyrinth with high walls and narrow corridors with potentially ominous consequences around the next corner.

COMPLEX

Complex changes are usually caused by many changes happening simultaneously. The multiple mazes merge into a larger, more complex maze. When your capacity to change is exceeded by more changes than you can handle, you run the risk of *hitting the wall*. Hitting the wall can be life threatening. It is like a juggler who can keep several balls in the air at the same time. Some jugglers are really good and can keep six or more going at the same time while others are less capable and can handle no more than three. But in both cases, there is a point where, if someone tosses another ball into the act, all the balls will fall.

This book will build toward navigating this larger and more complex change maze/labyrinth. There are ways to survive and even thrive when hitting the wall. But it requires more insight, strength, and purpose than you can muster by yourself.

FIGURE 1.3

NAVIGATION TIP:
The more you understand the kinds of mazes in front of you, the more prepared you are to navigate within them and through them.

Let's look at the RealityCase "Change in the Neighborhood" a bit further. My friend is faced with a blend of several change mazes: cultural—a growing and shifting urban environment, structural—the structure of roads and commerce, and personal—family growth, maturation, changing needs, conflicting activities.

Really, was any of this unpredictable? Which of these changes were desirable? Do you think he would have located in that comfortable little place in the suburbs if he had had any idea that all of these changes were going to happen? Do you think that maybe the desire for the positive change of moving to the suburbs might have caused him to ignore/deny future changes that were quite predictable?

Or was it the issue that it happened *too fast* (he figured it would happen but long after the kids left home or better yet, after he had retired)? These changes happened so fast (and subtly) that he was not prepared for them. So for him, the culture and structure changes were bad. As for the family that owned the farm across the road, they had tried to sell two years before he moved in, but they couldn't get their price. Finally they dropped the price a bit. A developer came along and bought the farm in time to pay for their kids' college educations. To them, the culture and structure changes were good.

Think about it. If the farmer would have sold two or three lots to friends who wanted to live in the country and kept on farming himself, the change wouldn't have been so great. But he sold the whole farm and 45 homes went into the development. When this was multiplied up and down the state road, the change really had an impact on the culture, which led to an impact on the structure, which led to the impact on my friend's life. Recognize that the change maze of a changing neighborhood can be viewed very differently by different parties.

There are a few fundamental facts about change that should be understood in order to help you shift from being overwhelmed and blindsided by the change maze you encounter to successfully coping and anticipating the change.

CHANGE MAZE SHAPERS

Why are some changes more traumatic than others? How about the opportunity that knocked but, since you didn't know how it would turn out, you didn't make the change? Can you identify a change that entered your life so fast that it almost blew you away but, looking back, you can see that it really wasn't such a big deal to navigate? Have you ever felt that things were going so well that you didn't want anything to change?

Several characteristics of change are what I call Maze Shapers. If you can identify these characteristics when you face a change maze or collection of mazes, it will go a long way to helping you figure out how to navigate successfully. These *shapers* are magnitude, risk & uncertainty, rate of change, and success.

MAGNITUDE

– the intensity of the change. How forceful is the change? How strong is the impact on you? Is it certain, non-negotiable, non-compromising, or is there room and time to alter its direction?

Since the attack on the World Trade Towers and the Pentagon in 2001, airline security procedures have been dramatically beefed up. The rules are clear and they are strongly enforced. I used to run to catch planes and arrive just before the aircraft door closed. No more! The change maze of security has become far more complex, time consuming, and frustrating. Nonetheless, the change has been made, and it is firm, so I've had to accept and adapt or I don't fly.

RISK AND UNCERTAINTY

– not knowing the outcome as you enter a change maze. If you have been confronted with a change and you are uncertain where it will lead, how do you react? What if you are trying to navigate through a change maze and there is high risk if you make a wrong decision? Are you afraid to move forward when you have no idea about the outcome of the possible decisions (turn right, left, go straight ahead, or freeze where you are in the midst of the change)?

Fear of failure often leads to being *risk averse*. When I first met Cheke (who is now my wife), I was unwilling to take the risk of asking her for a date because I was afraid she'd say no. I used the excuse that I didn't want to change from my "current state" of being single to a whole new paradigm. Fortunately, through the intervention of my Lord who used a good friend of mine, I finally took the risk. After 47 years of a marvelous God-led marriage, I'm so thankful that I was able to navigate that change.

RATE OF CHANGE

– how quickly has the change come on the scene? How well do you cope with change that jumps in your path quickly? Or how well do you handle changes that are moving faster than you think they should? What is your response when the school you attend or the company where you work passes new rules and puts them into effect immediately?

The shortage of crude oil and the war in the Middle East has sent the price of gasoline skyrocketing. Cheke and I examined our driving habits and our budget to navigate through a change maze we didn't like, but couldn't alter. Just about the time we became comfortable with our approach, Hurricane Katrina hit the gulf coast of the United States. The price of regular jumped from $2.51 to $2.59 yesterday. On the way home from a carefully planned shopping trip last evening, she suggested that I stop to fill the tank. I noticed that the tank was still a quarter full and since it had just gone up, I said I'd wait until today. By the time I stopped to get the tank filled this evening, our community had experienced two more increases from $2.79 to $2.99. The rate of change is seriously impacting our approach to this dynamic change maze (and our finances).

SUCCESS

– the *perception* of having everything under control and accomplishing your objectives. Have you been content with the status quo? What is your response when the elders at your church propose a new Sunday morning service format when the church is already growing at a comfortable pace? What is your opinion of the statement, "If it ain't broke, don't fix it"?

In my work with clients who want to improve, I've come to realize that the single biggest impediment to change is success. They are comfortable and don't want to do any more than tweak their approach to business and customers. Rather than make radical changes to move the firm into a more effective future, they will only go as far as embracing *better sameness*.

For a number of years, I worked for IBM. It was a dynamic, growing, and successful company. Frankly, I enjoyed being an "IBMer." After the Lord led me to a new profession, employer, and ministry field, I was able to watch IBM from outside the company. Over several years I observed that they were maintaining their same product line, their same marketing approach, their same level of customer service, and same pricing structure. After all, why change when they were so successful? Although some people thought it was quite sudden, competitors took over certain market segments; there were alternatives and much lower pricing for those same technologies. It took years for IBM to overcome its complacency and business arrogance. They had to replace their CEO and a number of top executives in order to *think new thoughts* and even scuttle some of their successful product lines and move into new ones. Their willingness to introduce severe change mazes turned them around (at a high cost to their staff, their customers, their profits, and their reputation). Not all of corporate America has learned that lesson, and bankruptcy is often the result.

I recommend a challenging little book that I often use in my consulting, *If It Ain't Broke, Break It,* by Robert J. Kriegel and Louis Patler. It really challenges the complacency of success.

NAVIGATION TIP:

If the change isn't really major in your life, if it represents low risk, and if it comes so slowly that you can see the details, don't get in a lather about it.

Table 1.4 lists key types of change mazes and concepts we face in our lifetime and gives descriptions that are relevant to learning to navigate through them.

TERM	CHANGE CONCEPTS 101
Continuous Change	Prolonged change without interruption
Sporadic Change	Change that occurs at irregular intervals and has no pattern or order
Predictable Change	Change that can be anticipated in advance and is often inevitable
Blind-Side Change	Change that is a complete surprise; sudden
Traumatic Change	Change that causes emotional upset and may even cause physical harm
Subtle Change	Change that is so slight that it is difficult to detect or analyze
Rate of Change	The speed at which change occurs
Accelerated Change	Increasing rate of change; change that occurs sooner than expected
Magnitude of Change	The size, extent, significance, or degree of impact caused by the change
Complex Change	Change that is made up of multiple, involved, and complicated changes that happen simultaneously

TABLE 1.4

CHAPTER TWO
Change Dimensions
and Changer Types

TWO DIMENSIONS OF CHANGE: FACTS AND EMOTIONS

When was the last time you encountered a change that got you either upset or really thrilled? Did it turn out as bad as you thought it would or as good as you anticipated? How careful were you to get the facts about the change before you let your emotions dictate your reaction? Have you ever had a close friend or spouse or parent or boss tells you to "calm down and think it through before you respond"?

Consider two *change dimensions*, two aspects of our humanity that are involved in change: the mind and the heart. Our minds apprehend the *facts* of the change and our hearts apprehend the *emotional impact and consequences* of the change. When you are faced with a change maze, these two dimensions can drive your actions and reactions, bring about joy or despair, create or destroy your creature comforts, determine sound or dysfunctional relationships, and foster delight or dread about facing the future. Here are some simplified descriptions that should help you distinguish these two change dimensions.

MIND

Facts; reality or the perception of reality; human senses; memory of the facts; what a person knows; system of reasoning; logic; mental skills

HEART

How a person feels; emotions; response to facts; how a person interprets facts or other emotions

As we progress through the book, we'll examine a third dimension that provides a whole new perspective when dealing with change: the soul (the spiritual aspect).

SOUL

Spiritual essence of a person; the inner vision that is able to keep eternity in view; the seat of faith, and hope in an afterlife (heaven and eternal life)

Imagine what it's like when you have a relationship with the Guide who views your change mazes from above and knows what lies around the corner, no matter how complex or how many. By seeing changes in the light of eternity as the Lord sees them, you'll gain a whole new approach to facing and navigating your change mazes.

But for now, in order to understand the way you respond to change from the mind and heart perspective, let's start by separating the *facts* from the *emotions*. The reality is that both dimensions come into play when you make your way through a change maze. The impact of change often causes conflicting signals for you, making navigation even more difficult (Figure 2.1). When both the facts and your emotions appear positive, you're pleased. But when they don't agree, you can lose your way in the maze. And if both are negative and yet you have to enter the maze, you can get overwhelmed.

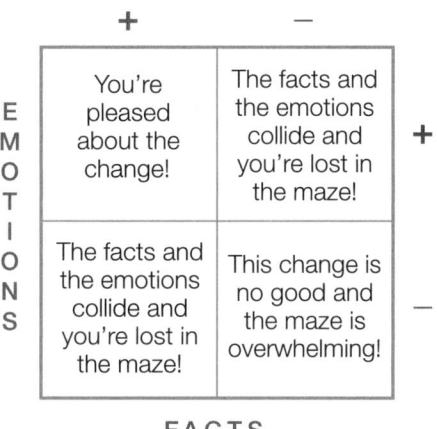

FIGURE 2.1

Let's be blunt! Although the facts may not change, your emotions strongly dictate how you'll face the maze. Change is usually not a problem if it goes your way! If the ground ball to the shortstop changes direction suddenly (due to a pebble in the infield grass) and the runner reaches on an error, you like that change if the runner is on *your* team. But if your team is in the field, you want new infield grass in time for the next game.

If the company decides to add a new level of management in your division and you're selected for the position, that's a stroke of genius by the board of directors. Yet if your work competitor gets the job . . .

One that's familiar to everyone—when you were 15 waiting to get your driver's license (at 16), the change of aging couldn't come fast enough. But at age 65, you'll do all kinds of things to try to put change on hold.

So the issue isn't the change itself as much as the emotional dimension, how the change *impacts* you. And impact is a perception, not necessarily a reality. Perception is primarily a heart (emotion) thing. The problem with perception is that it isn't necessarily based on facts. As the pages of this book unfold, you should be prepared to probe life's changes in a way that separates *what's changing* from *the change process* itself. Who knows? You may find that change sometimes is desirable. But going through the change process (the actual act of changing) is a bummer.

Many individuals understand opportunities, setbacks, and change in the workplace. Here is an example.

 RealityCase

Facing a Change Maze

Tanya had a master's degree in education, eight years experience as a successful fifth grade teacher, and had accomplished real results with kids and their parents as an elementary school principal. She was proud of the fact that their district had improved so much over the past four years. Tanya took delight in knowing they had pulled away academically and in sports from their rivals in the adjoining county (Branch) school district. Her husband drove 45 miles each way to his work, but he never complained and always said he'd support Tanya in whatever she wanted to do. Their two children, Wanda (9) and Bobby (7), enjoyed school, their neighborhood, town sports, and had a bunch of fun friends. Life was good.

On a Saturday morning in early March, just before heading to one of Bobby's baseball games, Tanya received a call from the chairman of the school board—in the county next door. "Tanya, we hear so many good things about your role as an educator, your leadership at the elementary school where you are principal, and the respect the community has for you. You may know that our superintendent left (at our request) at the end of last month. We are without a leader. It is not a secret that our district is one of the poorest in the state. Our kids are near the bottom of the academic ladder. Branch County's school buildings are in terrible shape. People in the community, especially the parents, are apathetic about kids' learning."

> "At our board meeting last Tuesday night, we voted 5-4 to invite you to consider becoming our superintendent. We are prepared to offer you $3,000 a year more than you are making now. We just don't have any more money than that. And by the way, your superintendent, although she would hate to lose you, agreed to let us talk with you. She indicated that your school was running so well that the assistant principal under you could run your school until the end of the year. That means we'd do everything we can to get you here by the first of April. What do you think?"
>
> Tanya's first impulse was, "No way!" But she does thrive on challenges.

One of the tools in facing a decision is to build a chart listing the pluses and minuses. Another is demonstrated with a simplified example of Tanya's *Change Chart*.

FACTS (MIND)	EMOTIONS (HEART)
Tanya is considered to be successful in her present role and location	She is pleased with the results of her work and is proud of the success
Her husband is supportive & her kids are content	In her view, life is good where she is
Tanya is wanted by the school board in Branch County (but the vote was close)	She is pleased to be recognized as an educator, leader, and citizen
Branch County is an unsuccessful school district and they fired the last superintendent mid-term	Tanya is competitive and thrives on winning
Branch County has little money to pay for the position	The job is worth a whole lot more than they are offering
This is a serious challenge	Tanya thrives on challenges

CHART 2.2

> **NAVIGATION TIP:**
> Try to separate the facts from your emotions about the change. Note: it won't be easy because so many of the thoughts that fill your mind are screened, filtered, tainted, massaged, adapted, truncated, expanded, or biased by your emotions.

It isn't always easy to separate the facts from emotions when faced with change; especially if it requires a decision to change or not change. You must be brutally honest with yourself and willing to acknowledge the issues of your heart. We'll examine the *Change v. Not Change* decision process more completely in Chapter 11.

THE THIRD DIMENSION: SPIRITUAL

How do you respond to getting older? Is that a change you look forward to, or do you dread it? What kind of changes are you planning for yourself and/or your family? Are they long-range or immediate? What happens when your plans for change crash into someone else's agenda? Are you able to view changes based on your faith in God and hope for eternity, or is it more about you here and now?

God has a plan for your life and often uses change to teach you, guide you, grow you, and increase your reliance on Him. God's Word (The Bible) is filled with examples about how and why He actually changes your view of what is happening around you. Your response to change can be spearheaded by your heart, your mind, or your soul. If you let God inhabit your soul, the dominance of the Lord in your life can lead you to cope with the facts and emotions of a change more effectively.

Fast forward to a few years after Tanya had accepted the position in Branch County. I interviewed Tanya to try to understand her thinking that led to making the change.

 RealityCase

Facing a Change Maze
Part 2

Interviewer: Tanya, what ever possessed you to take the job in Branch County?

Tanya: Well, I weighed the facts, recognized the challenge and opportunity to make a difference, and realized that this was a marvelous opportunity to help children who were in serious need of help. Besides, I had always wanted to be a superintendent—just not in a troubled situation like they were in.

Interviewer: What kind of results have you had?

Tanya: The kids are in class now. Absenteeism is way down in the normal range. Test scores have improved over the four years I've been there to being better than the state average. We still have a long way to go, but I believe these children can actually achieve with the best in the country. We have top-notch principals in all three of our schools, and the teachers are excellent, and that means they have the hearts as well as the knowledge to be good teachers.

Interviewer: Compare your first year on the job with this, your fourth year.

Tanya: At the end of the first day as superintendent, I couldn't even talk to my husband. I was so upset, so discouraged, and whipping myself for being so stupid. In one day I was fed up with many of the principals, the teachers, the school board, the parents, and the county. The only glimmer was the kids. They really needed help. They weren't learning. Oh yes, kids always learn. But they sure weren't learning what was important to learn because the school system wasn't teaching them. Period!

Now there are still town folk who don't like me, some parents want me out of there because I believe A's are awfully hard to earn and F's are real. The school board is always fussing about me. In fact, I still get nervous on the second Tuesday of every month, thinking they'll fire me like they did the last one. But the children are succeeding!

Interviewer: We now understand a little bit about the AS-IS (the way it was in the beginning) and the TO-BE (the way it is turning out), but what did you do to make the transition?

Tanya: You need to understand! I had not really been trained to face these kinds of issues. University programs don't prepare education leaders to lead in such situations. But, I read my Bible every day in search of godly wisdom. And I start my day on my knees. Then I go to the office to do what God shows me to do. Why in the first two weeks, several teachers and a principal "retired". What confused me was how upset the parents got with what I did. They seemed to like the way their kids weren't learning. At the first monthly meeting of the Board of Education they voted 5-4 to keep me. We cleaned house, set up the rules, and found teachers that knew their stuff and loved the kids.

Interviewer: Wait a minute. You introduced a new issue here. You said you prayed. Listening to you, your compassion, your excitement about the successes, the kids—I sense that you might have felt you were called to this position. You impress me as a called person.

Tanya: You seem to be getting it! I didn't want that job. Yes, I wanted to be a superintendent some day, but not be a miracle worker. The facts said, "Don't take it." Even my emotions about a challenge and all said, "Don't take it." That Saturday night after they called me, I decided on the spot to say no. But all day Sunday I asked the Lord what He wanted me to do. And I didn't have any peace about it until late Sunday night when I finally said yes. It even surprised me when I

> told them yes. Why even our children said a move would be fun. It was only 30 miles away so they could see their friends once in a while. You see, I don't work for the school system. I work for my Lord and if He says, "Change," I know I had better change. He'll take care of the rest.

This real life example, including the interview, brings the soul dimension into the picture. It causes the Christ-follower to add a third column to the Change Chart. What does God want you to do? Is His hand in it? Will He go before you into the high risk, uncertain change? Will the Lord show you the turns to take through the maze?

In fact, committed Christ-followers let the soul dominate their thinking and their emotions. God certainly has made humankind to have memories, reasoning powers, logic, common sense, and feelings. But He also provides the dominant force in change—*His will*—for His followers. Facts are important. Emotions are often even more important. But the soul dimension under the Lord's direction can provide the drive to change, the guidance through the change maze, the calm over change, the hope for change, and the satisfaction from change—no matter what the mind says and the heart desires.

NAVIGATION TIP:
God not only brings an eternal perspective to the situation, He knows what's ahead. He has the map to take you through the maze and is anxious for you to rely on Him for navigation.

When He was on earth, Jesus met a man named Zacchaeus (call him Zach). He worked for the tax service and in those days, tax agents could pocket any overcharge they could get by with (and Zach got more than his honest share). Jesus looked him in the eye and said, "I'm coming to your house for dinner tonight." And Zach agreed—happily. Can you imagine—a crooked tax agent welcoming *Jesus* into his house? The *facts* just don't fit. And Zach was excited about it! (What happened to his *emotions?*)

But the story doesn't stop there. Once Zach had an encounter with Jesus, he declared, "Lord half of my possessions I will give to the poor, and if I have defrauded anyone of anything, I will give back four times as much" (Luke 19:8). For the Christ-follower, all three change dimensions are at work, but the *soul* dimension becomes the dominant driver in the change.

Now that we've described the dimensions of change, it is important to look at different types of *changers*. Think of it this way. If you understand the interaction between you, the changer, and the change itself, you'll be able to determine your own unique approach to dealing with the change.

We'll take a look at how Change Shapers impact a maze after we've examined *Changers* themselves.

CHANGER TYPES:
FROM INNOVATOR TO RESISTOR

Do you know someone who really doesn't like to make changes? On the other hand, do you have a friend that just about wears you out with new ideas every time you get together? Has your family ever had to move to a new place and one member of your family just would not cooperate? Are you one of those people who keep papers in a file at work even though the company insists that you do everything on computers and store documents electronically?

Different people have different *change capacities*. Figure 2.3 demonstrates the spectrum of a population from *status quo* people to *innovation* people; resistor to innovator. The "population" could be that of your town, your church, your school, your work place, or even your extended family. Our research with clients, school districts, and churches shows that most people fall into the *slow follower/fast follower* areas under the curve. There are fewer people at the ends of the distribution who are adamant resistors (the over-my-dead-body type) or real innovators (the incessant new idea personalities).

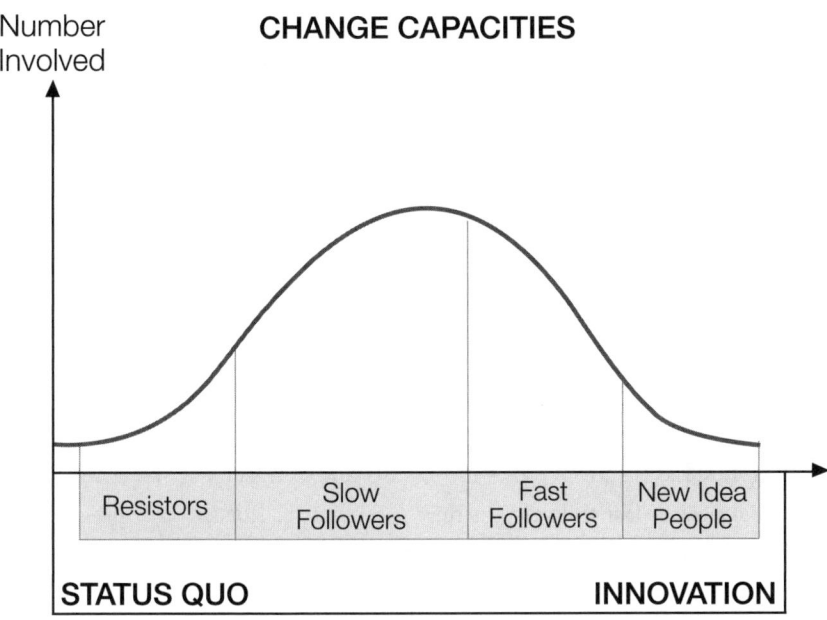

FIGURE 2.3

Be careful not to be too quick to label people you know as one of the types shown here. In fact, go slowly in categorizing yourself! Although certain personalities tend to fall into a particular area under the curve, external factors can cause an individual to move back and forth along the spectrum. *Change Capacity* is critical in determining your ability to cope with change and find your way through the maze.

CAPACITY	CHARACTERISTICS
Resistor	Does not like to change; is usually risk averse; feels comfortable with the status quo; looks more to the good old days than the future; often has a negative disposition
Slow Follower	Hesitates taking risks; is skeptical about change; needs strong evidence that the change will benefit him; wants others to make the change first; has a cautious disposition
Fast Follower	Is not an innovator; accepts change quickly once convinced it is beneficial; usually is a strong supporter of the change once into it; has a show-me disposition
New Idea Person	Looks at new ways to make things better; pushes for change; willingly takes risks; thrives on fast changes; has a make-it-happen disposition

TABLE 2.4

Everyone has a natural tendency toward one of the change capacities: resistor, slow follower, fast follower, or new idea person. But the change issue and the kind of maze may move you to the left or the right between the *status quo* and *innovation*.

NAVIGATION TIP:
Assess your capacity in the light of the change maze in front of you.

FACING THE CHANGE: FROM AS-IS TO TO-BE

What is the first question someone asks you when you call them for directions to the party at their house? Isn't it, "Where are you or where are you coming from?" Have you ever heard the expression, "If you don't know where you're going, any road will get you there"?

Transition is *moving* through a change maze. It is the actions required for you to pass through those corridors and take the turns that will get from the maze entrance to the exit.

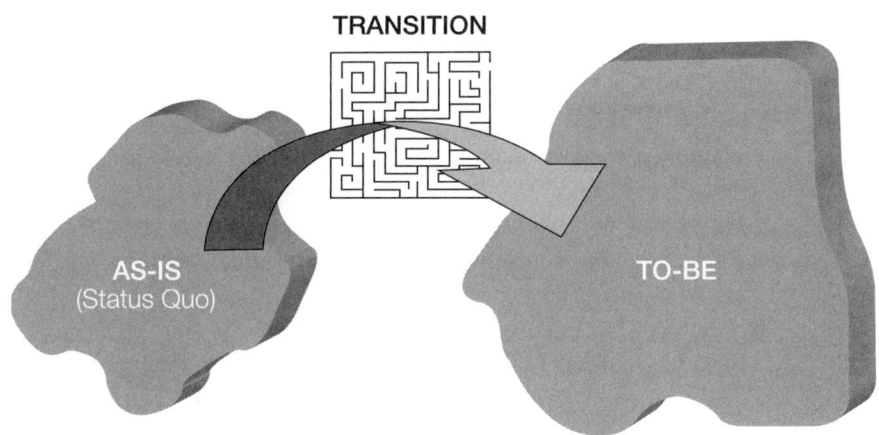

FIGURE 2.5

One of the difficulties in considering a change is that many times you haven't really determined the following key factors:

WHERE YOU ARE

Where you stand on the change. You may not even know the real details of what this change is about (known as the AS-IS stage).

WHAT'S SO GREAT ABOUT WHERE YOU ARE

Why you may want to hang on to the status quo (especially if you are comfortable with things just as they are).

WHAT'S SO GREAT ABOUT THE RESULT OF THE CHANGE

What the impact/outcome of the change might be on you (the TO-BE stage).

WHAT IT WOULD TAKE TO MAKE THE CHANGE

What you have to invest (time, energy, resources, etc.) to accommodate the change (TRANSITION stage).

WHETHER YOU OUGHT TO EMBRACE THIS CHANGE OR RESIST IT

Making a decision about whether to change or not.

WHERE YOU CAN FIND DIRECTION

The tools and map to navigate through the maze.

In many cases, even if the AS-IS is clear, the TRANSITION and TO-BE are filled with uncertainty. We discussed earlier the fact that most people do not like uncertainty. For the *risk averse* person, uncertainty is a strong excuse *NOT* to change. Together, uncertainty and fear of risk pose a serious impediment to making a change. If you think you're quite successful without the change and that the maze came too quickly, all of the ingredients to move you toward being a slow follower or even a resistor on the Change Capacities spectrum are there (Figure 2.6).

Even if you consider yourself to be an innovator or a fast follower, change mazes that are recognizably major (magnitude), filled with uncertainty (risk), and have come on the scene quickly (rate) may cause you to become a resistor or slow-follower.

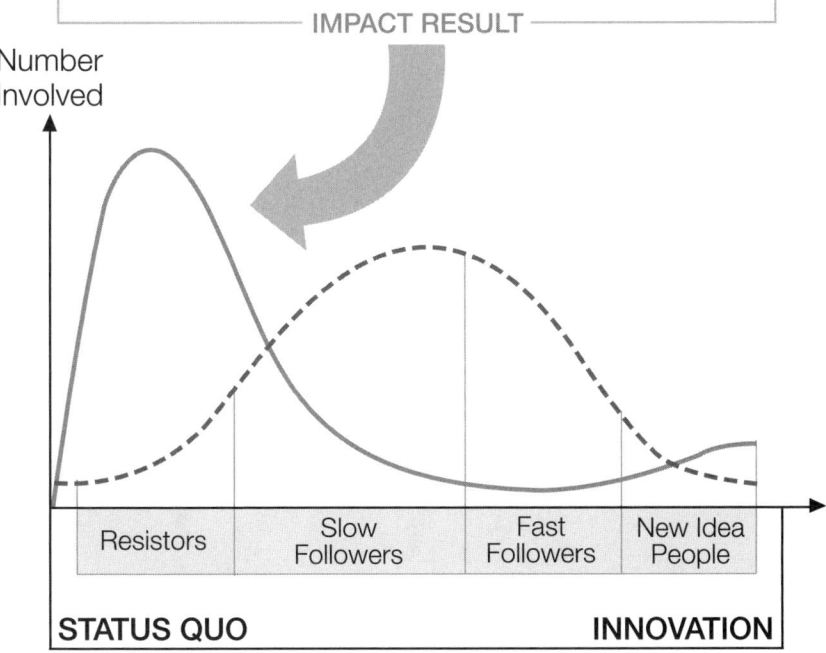

FIGURE 2.6

We've summarized several key concepts about the characteristics of change, the dimensions involved (heart, mind, soul), the spectrum of change capacities, and the impact of risk, uncertainty, rate, and success. You've even been given *nav tips* that should help you begin to navigate change mazes.

Now, how can you put that to work? What do you do when you're actually facing a change that you don't understand or like or know the outcome of or that messes with your successes or threatens your status quo, or that you simply can't control?

The following ✓LIST is designed to help you turn concepts into reality when you are actually facing a change.

NAVIGATION ✓LIST 1

QUESTIONS	COMMENTS	YOUR RESPONSE
Just what is the change confronting you?	Describe the change in factual, realistic terms–not emotional responses.	
Are you pleased/upset because there is a change at all and you've made up your mind that you do/don't like change—period?	Try to determine your attitude about change—do you naturally resist change or are you willing to be open about change?	
Which of the change concepts applies for this change maze?	Hint: See Table 1.4 and try to list them all (there is usually more than one).	
What are the facts about your current state (AS-IS)?	Be sure to stick to the facts!	
What do you think will be the results of making this change (TO-BE)?	What are the facts and what is speculation?	
What are your feelings (emotions) about this change?	Be honest with yourself. No one else needs to see your answers.	
What are the risks of personal failure? Are you more comfortable without the change (you prefer the status quo)? How certain are you that this will work? Did this change maze jump in front of you too quickly? Do you consider this change to be difficult?	Identify and describe the Change Shapers.	
For this change maze, where are you on the Change Capacity Spectrum?	Is this where you would normally place yourself or have the Change Shapers impacted where you are?	

QUESTIONS	COMMENTS	YOUR RESPONSE
Does this change impact you for good or for bad? Explain how.	This is tough to do without a personal foundation—core values & basic beliefs—to determine good and bad.	
What are the spiritual implications of this change?	Describe the soul dimension.	
Have you prayed about this change and what your response should be to it?	This could be your most powerful navigation tool.	
Now here are the tough questions. Who, besides you, is impacted by the change? Is that good or bad in your opinion?	This requires thinking outside yourself and should include the proponents of the change as well as those who have no say in its happening but will feel its impact.	
Did this whole change catch you by surprise or can you honestly say you saw it coming?	Often people see it coming, but deliberately choose to deny that the change will happen.	
Now, whether you consider the change bad or good, how can you use it for your good or the good of others? What constructive actions can you take to benefit from the change and improve the change?	Accept that the change will happen. Don't argue with it anymore. Instead how can it benefit you or your colleagues or family?	
For this change confronting you now, what will it take to shift your attitude to the right on the Change Capacity scale? Or is this a non-negotiable change that you should resist with all your mind, heart, and soul?	List actions and attitudes that will help you move to the right (if the change is constructive or inevitable)—or take a stand against the change (if it is destructive).	

Below are a few fundamentals about change that should help you to shift from being overwhelmed to successfully navigating the change mazes you encounter.

CHANGE FUNDAMENTALS

1 The rate of change in the world is accelerating and becoming more sporadic (discontinuous).

2 The growing magnitude of change is amplified by increasing complexities.

3 People often apply "better sameness" in an effort to avoid required change.

4 Change abides by the law of inertia (If a body is at rest or moving at constant speed in a straight line, it will continue to do so unless it is acted upon by a force).

5 The spectrum of capacities for change ranges from resistors to new idea people.

SECTION 1 PonderPoints

The following questions are intended to help you internalize concepts discussed in Section I. Think them through. You may want to begin a journal of both exciting and troubling ideas to help you navigate change mazes in your future.

1. Identify three change mazes that made a significant impact on your life.

2. Complete the following table about those three changes.

DESCRIPTION OF THE MAZE	TYPE OF CHANGE (CHECK ALL THAT APPLY)	CHANGE FACTS	YOUR EMOTIONS AT THE TIME
	__ Planned __ Predictable __ Traumatic __ Continuous __ Sporadic __ Subtle		
	__ Planned __ Predictable __ Traumatic __ Continuous __ Sporadic __ Subtle		
	__ Planned __ Predictable __ Traumatic __ Continuous __ Sporadic __ Subtle		

3. Describe how God has used each of those three mazes to shape your life.

4. Can you remember a change in your life that caused you serious trauma because it was all about you? Describe it. Would it have been less traumatic if you had considered the Lord's perspective instead of your own?

5. Consider your personality and attitudes. Where do you fit generally on the Change Capacity Spectrum: Resistor, Slow Follower, Fast Follower, or Innovator? Relate an experience where change happened and God asked you to shift one way or the other.

6. Describe the magnitude and risk to you of the 9/11 terrorist attack.

7. How has 9/11 impacted your plans for the future? What can you do to shift more of your thinking about the event to a spiritual view?

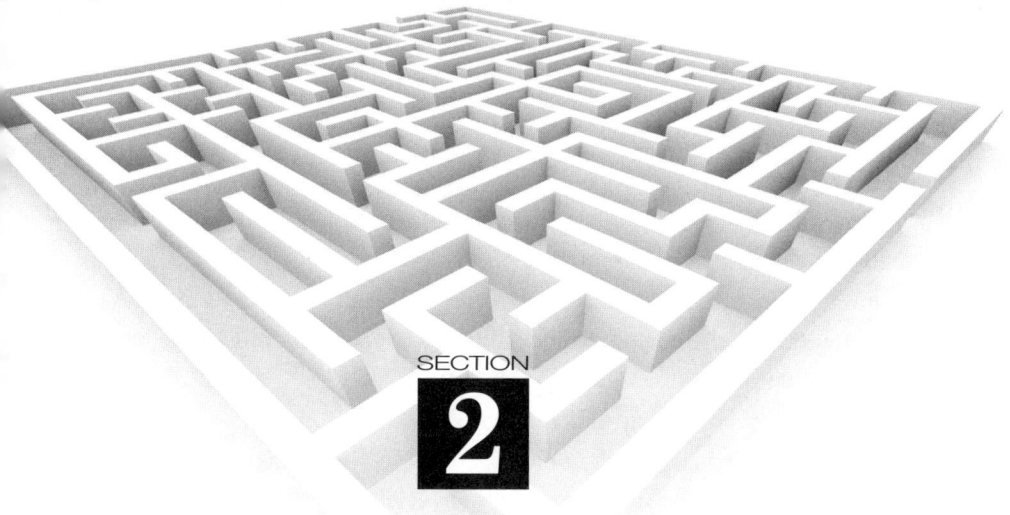

SECTION 2

YOUR PERSONAL NAVIGATION KIT:
a way of life

Managing yourself when you are faced with a change maze is a process and a way to think, not a formula with a prescriptive set of rules. Your navigation kit should be filled with processes that fit you and strategies for using them. These processes can be built and continually honed by you based on your successful and unsuccessful change experiences. This section examines the characteristics of each change type and describes ways to think about them that I have found useful. Examples are designed to help you relate these concepts to actual change mazes in order to add processes and strategies to your navigation kit. Later in the book we'll deal with the cases where God convinces you to resist entering a particular change maze or where He has given you insights that cause you to stand against foreboding change.

The least threatening type of change is usually predictable change, providing you acknowledge that it's there. A close second is planned change, especially if it is the result of your own plans. If you don't take the energy to consider them as changes at all, you could be surrounded by dead ends and wrong turns. Frankly, predictable changes are often not worth resisting. They are usually inevitable.

We'll then move on to the characteristics of sporadic and blind-side changes. In these cases, the simple maze becomes more complex and the navigation tools you adopt will usually require more effort and faster response. The magnitude and the rate of change may make it seem like you are trying to find your way through a maze in the dark.

Finally we'll wrap up this section by taking a sobering look at traumatic change, where the maze becomes a complex 3-dimensional labyrinth with threatening walls in front of you and walls closing in from the sides.

CHAPTER THREE
Navigating Changes
You Know Are Coming

The Lord God commanded the man, saying, "From any tree of the garden you may eat freely; but from the tree of the knowledge of good and evil you shall not eat, for in the day that you eat from it you will surely die." (Genesis 2:16–17)

Name some changes in your life that were so subtle and so continuous that you didn't really think of them as changes. What are some of the predictable changes that occur to a young person and the family after he or she finishes high school? How have you or your family planned for the predictable changes that are ahead for you?

Looking ahead and planning for predictable changes will help you avoid some of the risks of taking wrong turns in the change maze. It all sounds simple, but for many, denial and procrastination can make the predictable change yield serious consequences. Think about hurricane Katrina that hit the southern United States in 2005. There were clear predictions that a major change was on the way. But many people chose to deny that it was coming, misjudging both its magnitude and its speed. Others weighed the information, set aside their emotional urge to hang onto their current circumstances, and planned to get out of the way. Denial and procrastination cost people their lives. That is not to say that everyone could make a change. Some knew it would be tragic but, because they were infirm or too poor or trapped, couldn't get out. There are times when you know you need to change but don't have the power to do it.

It is critical that you separate the way change hits from the change itself. You may be more accepting of predictable changes because they are subtle and continuous even if the outcome is not good.

For example:

TERM	CHANGE CONCEPTS 101
Continuous Change	Prolonged; change without interruption
Predictable Change	Anticipated in advance and may be considered to be inevitable even when it isn't
Subtle Change	So slight that it is difficult to detect or analyze

TABLE 3.1

1 The growth of a person from birth to maturity is usually continuous. (For grandparents who don't see the grandkids very often, growth appears to be in steps instead. Have you ever heard, "Oh, how you've grown since we saw you last!"?)

2 When a woman first begins to show that she is pregnant and she adds weight, there are predictable changes. And after the birth, the growth of the child's height and weight is predictable. In fact, if those changes did not take place as predicted, there would be serious concern that the right changes weren't happening.

3 Once a man reaches late 20s or early 30s, a subtle change often occurs, adding a few pounds each year. The 140 pound groom can grow to 180 by the time he reaches the age of 55. Now if he wouldn't have added 1-2 pounds a year for 25 years . . .

Everything living—people, plants, animals, birds, fish, viruses, diseases—follows reasonably predictable stages of growth. These stages roll out in the shape of what is known as an S-Curve.

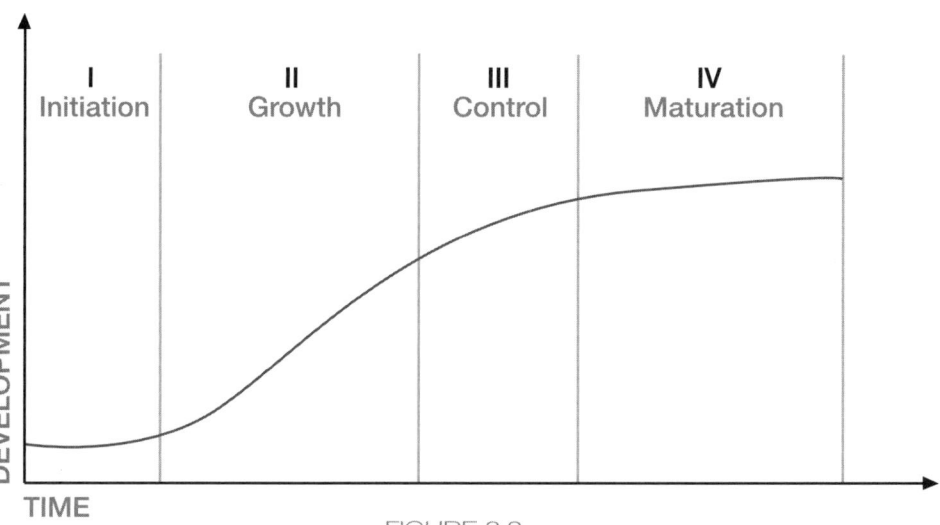

FIGURE 3.2

STAGE	NAME	CHARACTERISTICS
I	Initiation	Start, beginning, new idea, conception, birth
II	Growth	Contagion, expansion, excitement
III	Control	Slower growth, more deliberation, less risk taking
IV	Maturation	Slowing down, practicality, caution, aversion to change

TABLE 3.3

The key to dealing with the stages of growth is facing the reality that they are predictable. The fact that they are predictable is not necessarily good, but at least you usually know that each stage will happen.

Consider the woman who loves babies—the cuddling, the softness of their skin, the smell of the baby powder, and the cooing are all a delight. She may even say, "Oh, if they could just stay like that it would be wonderful." But like it or not, that sweet baby moves right on to the terrible twos and beyond. It is predictable!

Some people who do not like to think of a child growing up will try to dress the kid in clothes like a much-younger child. Or they will make sure the child doesn't play in the backyard without a parent near or won't let them sit in Sunday school without Mother. Even though the change is inevitable, a parent may choose to deny that change (even impede related predictable changes like emotional development). A recent phenomenon is called "helicopter parents"—they're the ones who check in with their college kid by cell phone morning, noon, and night and often call professors to find out how their child is performing.

Others may encourage and even push the change. The two-year-old is allowed to make a mess at the dinner table, he drinks from a big boy cup, and helps clear the dishes (plastic works better than china). Dad thrills to see his son throw the ball like a five-year-old when the child is only three. And since this growth is predictable, Mom is already looking at sale clothes two years in advance with the idea that "he'll grow into them."

> **NAVIGATION TIP:**
> Keep your head up to see clearly those predictable changes that will impact you. Don't avoid or deny their existence.

Now let's look at planned change. If you are planning a change that impacts structure and culture in your life, you may become more comfortable because you feel more in control. In fact, you can also, through planning, attempt to manage the rate and magnitude of the change. (We'll hold the discussion about change that someone else plans that impacts you until later.)

How do you work your way through a change maze where a predictable change requires a planned change? Consider the family that owns and lives in a small, two-bedroom home on a tight-fitting lot. The S-Curve of Growth is introducing a change. The Lord has given them the delight of knowing a fourth child is on the way—a baby girl. And the other three are boys.

Joy, frustration, and concern all meet at the kitchen table when the wife/mom announces that something has to give. They've had difficulty cramming three young boys (ages 7, 4, and 2) into one bedroom, and Mom and Dad can't share their bedroom with a new baby for more than a few months. As the discussion continues into the night after the boys are in bed, they admit that in terms of the growth curve, the house and lot have reached maturity. They can't expand on the lot because they are already at the edges, and they can't build up (add a story) because the structure of the house can't handle it.

The man of the house has a good position at work, and they have a sound savings account. The solution is to move from the predictable change to a more planned change. They decide to sell their present house (the neighbor next door will probably buy it because he wants more yard space for his kids) and build a new one in a growing subdivision at the edge of town.

As they complete the deal with the developer, architect, and bank, the frustration and concern turn to confidence, excitement, and relief. Dad and Mom are now in control of the planned change. Since they have laid out the schedule for selling, building, and moving, it appears that the rate of change is under control. Considering the size of the new house, the cost, and the design, the magnitude of the change is under their control as well.

> **NAVIGATION TIP:**
> Do an ongoing assessment of a predictable change in your life. It should lead you to strategies that will help you navigate the maze more effectively and help you keep your cool.

Section 2 Chapter 3 PonderPoints

1. Indicate where you are on the S-Curve for the different areas of your life. Write each of the letters from the following list on the curve shown on the next page.

    A Physical

    S Spiritual

    P Professional

    E Emotional

    R Relational (where you are with your closest friends)

    F Financial (where you think you are in managing your finances)

    B Balance (where you are in getting the various aspects of your life (spiritual, family, profession, etc.) in balance.

    For example, if you have been growing in your ability to develop friendships and now are working to make them more lasting by controlling your emotional swings, your might put an "R" in the control stage.

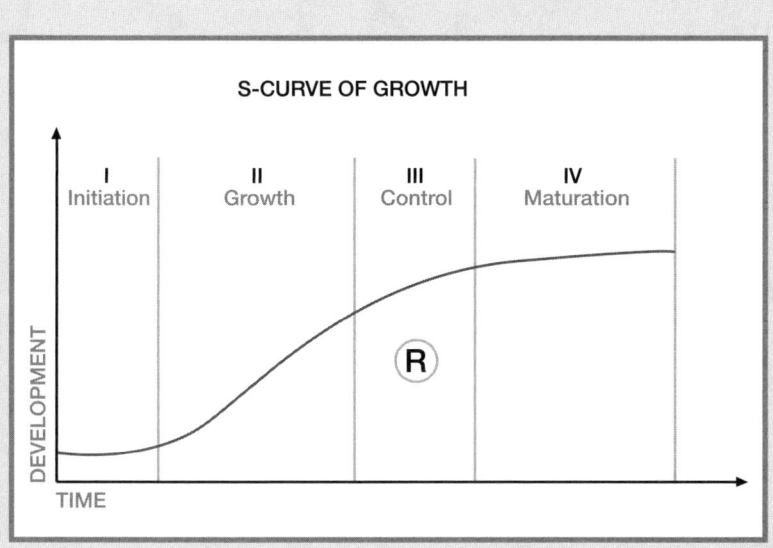

2. Identify one of the stages on the S-Curve of Growth where you have the most concern. Develop a plan that could help you through that predictable change.

CHAPTER FOUR
Understanding
the Birth/Growing/Aging/Death Life-Cycle

If you are a teenager, do you pay much attention to where you are in your Stages of Growth? If you're a parent or grandparent, are you interested and maybe even concerned about the stages of your children or grandchildren? What should you do if you have children who don't seem to care at all about the changes ahead—changes you can predict? When you speed while driving in a heavily patrolled area, are you really surprised when your plans get changed as the police pull you over? What does God's Word say about the predictable consequences of certain actions?

Genesis 2:16–17 (See the beginning of Chapter 3 to refresh your memory) records a command that God gave to Adam and Eve. Did they face a predictable change? It may not have been to their liking, but God's rules and promises go beyond predictable—they are certain. Read the scripture closely—notice that God did not say if. Instead He said when.

Since the fall of man in the Garden of Eden recorded in Genesis, there has been a back-side extension to the S-Curve. As a result of His plan and their response, God added Stages V & VI, decay and termination (death). This complete change spectrum from initiation (conception) to termination (death) is referred to as the life-cycle.

STAGE	NAME	CHARACTERISTICS
V	Decay	Aging, contraction, disappointment
VI	Termination	Death, closing, passing on, destruction

TABLE 4.1

For the individual, these last two stages of decay and death are predictable changes that are usually resisted, denied, and/or ignored. But you can be sure that whatever is born physically ultimately dies physically (until God changes all of that with Christ's second coming to earth). Figure 4.2 shows all of the stages from initiation to termination.

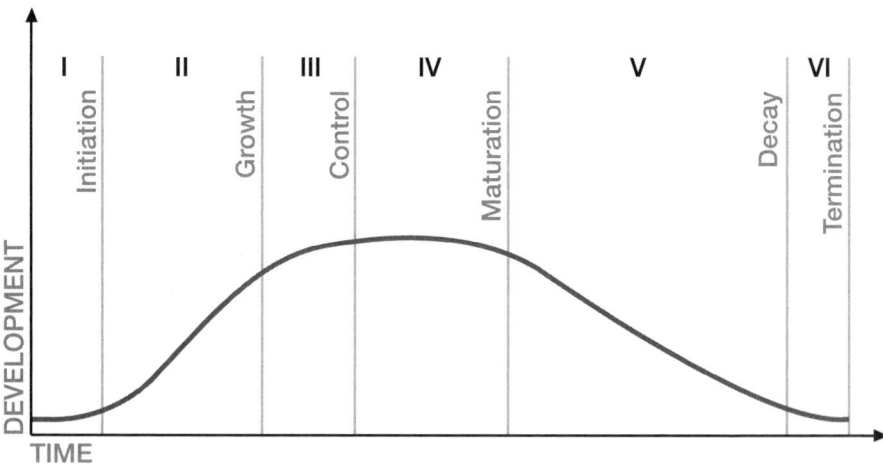

FIGURE 4.2

It is easy to see how the Stages of Growth & Decay is often called the life-cycle because they refer to living organisms. The term "living organism" can be applied beyond humans, plants, animals, fish, and foul. Consider businesses, institutions of learning, governments (and nations), churches, denominations, religions, ideas, buildings, cities, vehicles, roads, technologies, rules of law, stars (according to most astronomers), glaciers . . . The life-cycle can be applied to these as well—providing an understanding that gives the individual a valuable tool to anticipate, cope, use, and sometimes alter predictable change.

As mentioned before, both the change itself and the way the change occurs (or is presented) are critical to dealing with it. Read the following RealityCase about my wife (Cheke), her parents, and the Lord. Identify the following:

1 Predictable changes
2 Magnitude of the changes
3 Rate of changes

RealityCase

Life's Bumps in the Road

Cheke was really upset. In fact, she was ticked off with the whole deal. And her mom and dad didn't seem to understand that she didn't want to move. Especially to that town in the middle of Nowhere South Dakota. Here she was—just about to start her sophomore year in high school. Cheke was a superb student, she was first chair in the clarinet section of the high school band, had great friends, was active in the church youth group, and had settled in to use and enjoy the city's cultural features: the symphony, the library, the museums.

Paul, her dad, was a minister. In the denomination where he pastored, the district superintendent decided who went where. And he seemed to like to play musical chairs with the ministers in his district. Each spring at the annual conference, he'd recommend to the denominational board who should move and where they should go. And that board had done nothing more than rubber-stamp his plans since they had put him in office. All the preachers' kids hated it. Some would get to stay and others had to move–in the spring right after school was out.

Well, Cheke's folks had just returned from conference with the word – move to Nowhere South Dakota, a town of 550 people, 7,000 cats and dogs, 350 pickup trucks, two grocery stores, one high school, a run-down train station, a grain elevator, a bar and pool hall, a gas station, Coast-to-Coast hardware store, Olsen's Dairy, Lena's Chat & Chew, and Clement's Chevrolet.

Fortunately (for dad), Cheke's mom, Mabel, was a godly woman. She and Paul prayed a lot, and they trusted the Lord, so she supported him all the way. "God's will isn't always what we want, but Scripture says that 'everything works out for good for those who love and serve the Lord' and we sure do love and serve Him."

So off they went to Nowhere. Cheke didn't enjoy it much, but things seemed to work out okay. She played in the school's small band, ended up in the All-State Band two years in a row, continued to play the piano, especially in church, was the superintendent of Bible School each year, and earned a couple of scholarships to college.

Finally, Cheke got to leave Nowhere. She went to college. It was a sad day for mom and dad but a really happy day for her. She sang in the choir, played in the college orchestra, and got involved in Inter-Varsity with a great bunch of Christians. Oh, by the way, she also got better than good grades as she prepared to teach elementary kids.

And then it happened! At Inter-Varsity one night she met a guy who was turned on for the Lord. Before long they began to date pretty regularly. Mabel wasn't too sure about the guy; called him an eager beaver, but both Paul and Mabel knew they couldn't control Cheke from miles away, so they prayed and left her in the Lord's hands.

Well, after a few years, Cheke married the guy–me. And the first thing we did was move much further away from Nowhere for me to finish my degree and for Cheke to teach.

After I graduated, I went to work for a big corporation and moved her still further away from her mom and dad. In fact, Mabel told me, "You really don't want to take that kind of job and move so far away." I was usually polite but also direct: "Mom, you're wrong! I do want to take that job and go wherever they want me. I think you're speaking for yourself. It's you who doesn't want me to take the job and move so far away." She laughed and then agreed.

Cheke and I built a comfortable little home in the city 400 miles away. We were really hoping to start a family but God had other ideas for that time in our life. Several miscarriages proved that. But I was successful in the business world and Cheke got involved in Women's Bible Studies and at church. Together, we taught a high school Sunday school class—and get this—we learned an awful lot about the Word from the kids. Those teenagers were sharp and strong believers.[1]

And then change hit again. The district superintendent decided it was time for Paul and Mabel to move from Nowhere to another church. And the assignment was to Further Nowhere, North Dakota. Paul agonized over the assignment. If only they were younger (he was now in his 60s), he'd do it without a second thought. God had always cared for them and this would be no exception. But after earnest, heavyhearted prayer, he actually refused to take the assignment! The superintendent recommended to the rubber-stamp board that Paul be relieved of his church and out within 30 days.

Well, Paul and Mabel had a problem. They had no home, had never been part of a pension plan—not even Social Security. The only things they owned (and Paul claimed it was really the Lord's) was a tired old car, a piano, and some furniture and household goods. Paul tried to negotiate and prayed, but the superintendent wouldn't give an inch. In fact, the new minister was scheduled to arrive at the end of the 30 days. Paul and Mabel had to get out. But where would they go?

A thousand miles away, Paul's younger brother, Buck, owned a large and successful car dealership. When Buck heard about Paul's

---

[1] Ten years later 12 of the 14 kids in that class were in vocational Christian service.

problem, he called. "Get rid of your furniture and come live with us. You can work for me." Mabel was willing, as always, but she just couldn't face losing the piano and what little furniture they had.

Paul was hesitant, and he delayed–until the new preacher and his furniture showed up at the front door. "Give me a day and I'll be out of here." The new minister agreed and Paul found one of his farmer church members (Charlie) who would loan him his truck–and some strong backs to load it.

As they were loading, Charlie said, "Paul, where are you taking this stuff?" "I don't know, but God has never let me down, and he won't now." By late afternoon the truck was loaded. Then the phone rang. It was Cheke. "Dad, our city is right between your place and Uncle Buck's. We have an empty basement, and a great place in the living room for mom's piano. Bring your belongings here. We'll take care of them as long as you like, and when you need them in the future, we'll get them to you."

Paul just smiled. "God does provide–but I just found out there is a problem. We have to unload this truck and have it back to Charlie by tomorrow night. We can't make it that fast!" Then I got on the phone. "You can make it! Drive here, we'll unload it while you rest, and then you can get it back in time." And guess what, it worked.

But what about Paul and Mabel's future? Well, God really used Buck. When Buck, the consummate businessman, found out that Paul had no retirement, no home, and no savings, he took action. "Paul, besides being a good preacher, you're a super mechanic. Now a man your age shouldn't have to grease cars and repair engines. You're also a dear man of God. Why don't you clean up cars and keep an eye on our service department? The men will know you're my brother and they'll soon know that you're a trusted and loving believer in Jesus Christ. And if you can work for me for at least five years, we'll make sure your Social Security is up-to-date, and you'll have some savings and a little pension."

Well, Paul worked for Buck for more than 10 years–well into his seventies. Buck's health insurance plan even helped with illness that

> Mabel encountered along the way: cancer. Many people thought it was good doctors that made her whole again, but Paul and Mabel knew that it was really the work of a loving Lord. He always had taken care of them.
>
> They finally retired in a low income retirement complex that Mabel said was the most beautiful place she'd ever lived. The kids outfitted the place with totally new furniture. Paul couldn't believe that he could watch a clear picture on a color 27-inch TV from a real leather recliner—and Mabel could write in her diary at a solid oak desk.
>
> He went to be with the Lord at 87 and Mabel stayed around until she was 91.
>
> Both of them were living proof that the changes that happen through life–when you depend on Him who knows and plans your steps–were perfect (but sometimes difficult).
>
> And what about Uncle Buck? He died a terribly poor man (financially). The business went bankrupt. But he died a blessed rich man (spiritually).

Changes, even life-cycle changes, are complex. Notice in the RealityCase that several life-cycles were involved and interrelated: Cheke's, mine, Paul's and Mabel's, and even Buck's. Only God is capable of orchestrating all of them at the same time. Here are two verses of encouragement from the pages of scripture that tell about His involvement in our changes.

> Man's steps are ordained by the Lord. How then can man understand his way? **Proverbs 20:24**

> And we know that God causes all things to work together for good to those who love God, to those who are called according to His purpose. **Romans 8:28**

This sobering discussion of life's cycles is not intended to be fatalistic or discouraging. But acknowledging the realities of the life-cycle's predictable change should lead to planned change. If you acknowledge life-cycle and other predictable changes and want to do something about them, here are several alternative ways to deal with the maze.

1. Do nothing and let it happen. (What has the greater risk; ignoring it or taking some kind of action?)

2. Plan changes that will thwart the prediction or at least delay it. (Are you able to adjust the maze to make it more solvable?)

3. Plan for new changes that will compensate for and/or take advantage of the predicted change. (If you accept the maze, can you create another maze that will offset the one in front of you?)

For instance, with carefully planned changes, you can often prolong your body's life-cycle. It can be honed through the discipline of a healthy lifestyle including exercise, wise eating, constructive relationships, refraining from drug abuse, etc. Research has shown that the mind is kept strong by continued, disciplined learning. A healthy heart, with well-managed emotions, leads to less stress, sound relationships, added resilience, and more. And a vibrant soul that is Christ-centered instead of self-centered results in a peace and contentment that promotes spiritual, emotional, and physical health.

A SPECIAL NOTE: The Decay and Termination Stages never happen for the soul! And during the life of a sold-out Christ-follower, the spiritual Growth Stage never stops! As Paul writes to the Philippians, "For to me, to live is Christ and to die is gain." The Christian's life-cycle never ends because he has been given Eternal Life through Christ. A graph cannot accurately depict the eternal life of your soul but it can show its relationship to the finiteness of the mind and heart. (See Figure 4.3.)

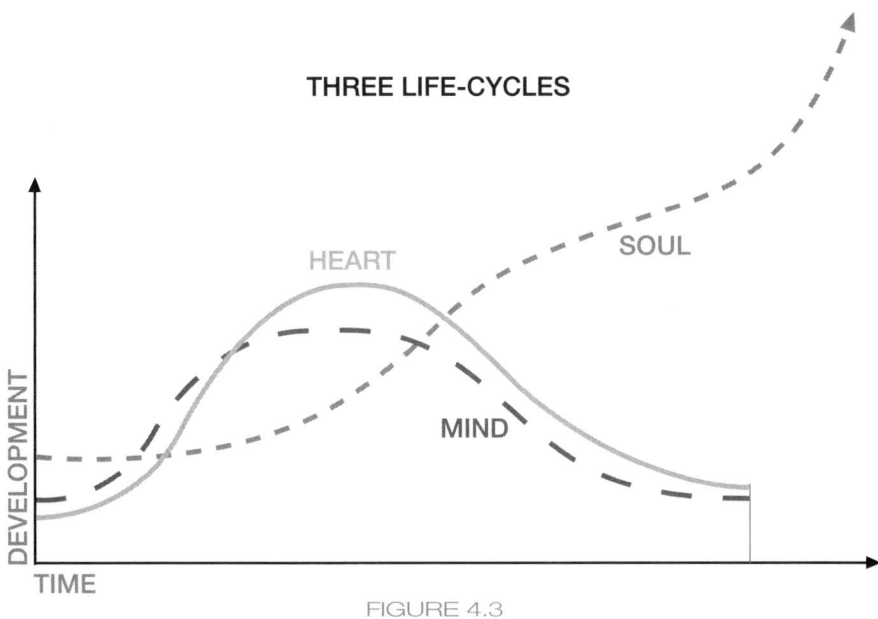

FIGURE 4.3

The term "everlasting life" in the Bible refers to the fact that your soul lives beyond the mortal life-cycle of the physical body, mind, and heart. It is truly eternal.

Section 2 Chapter 4 PonderPoints

1. Identify three changes that you are involved in right now and that you consider to have been predictable.

2. Mark on the following graph which stage each of the changes you identified is in.

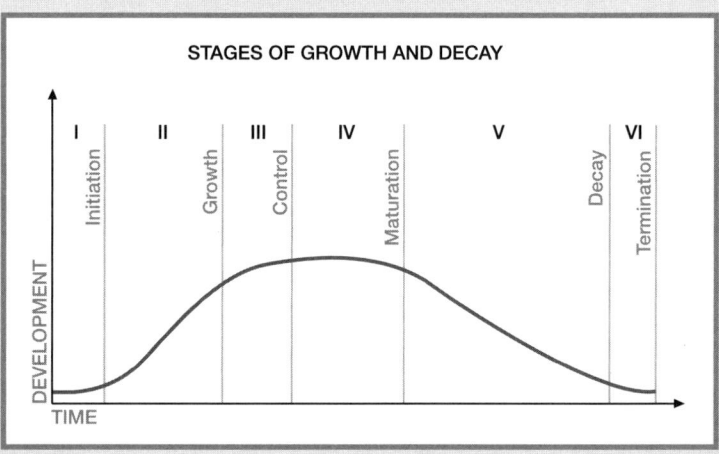

CHAPTER FIVE
Planning Changes:
Blending the Predictable with Your Agendas

Have you, or someone you know, insisted on knowing the results of a prenatal ultrasound that tells the gender of an unborn child so that you would know what color to paint the baby's room? What plans do you have to extend your life or at least stay healthy longer? How do you plan in advance for the offering you want to give to the Lord when you know that a tough financial month is coming? What are you doing to plan your finances for when you retire? If you are already retired, how are you planning to expend your resources? Do you have a written will?

Even if you are not a planner, there are several steps you can take to reduce the risk of predictable changes turning into traumatic and troublesome changes. Recognize also that there are cases where planning may get you into a maze you can't get out of. Consider a rich man described in the Scriptures.

> The land of a rich man was very productive. And he began reasoning to himself, saying, "What shall I do, since I have no place to store my crops?" Then he said, "This is what I will do: I will tear down my barns and build larger ones, and there I will store all my grain and my goods. And I will say to my soul, 'Soul, you have many goods laid up for many years to come; take your ease, eat, drink and be merry.'"
>
> But God said to him, "You fool! This very night your soul is required of you; and now who will own what you have prepared?" Luke 12:16–20

What happened here? Identify the man's mind issues and his heart perspective. Jesus, the speaker here, even called him a fool. It certainly wasn't because the rich man planned. He even planned for his retirement ("I'll have plenty of good things laid up for many years"). It was because he failed to make plans regarding soul issues—the eternity view.

Did your mom and dad set goals for you? Have you set high achievement goals for your sons and daughters at an early age? Some people have plans for their children so far in advance that bank accounts, baby room colors, toy boxes full of educational toys, music box selections, even pre-registration at nursery school or daycare are put in place before the child is even born. And after birth, if Mom and Dad don't do the planning, grandparents do! Visions of sports success, drama and music fame, pre-registration in college alma mater grandkid programs, and pushing for careers based on parent/grandparent choices are topics for long discussions at the family dinner table while the child is off exploring grandmother's suitcase. You may want to think twice before you plan life-changes for someone else, even for your kids.

Our studies[2] show that university and career goals set by parents/grandparents can undermine the talents and aspirations that God has built into a person's capabilities and personality. And the pressure can be so great to achieve what mom and dad have planned that change is almost impossible or is viewed as rebellion. The result can be unhappiness throughout their lives and/or depression and/or professional failure and/or even suicide.

But what if you're goal oriented? Is there a contradiction between being goal oriented and thriving in a changing world? Not necessarily if you're willing to allow changes in your goals that God puts in place as He grows you. Be sure to establish life goals consistent with God's direction in your life. Look beyond your own ambitions and prayerfully consider other people as well: spouse, family, brothers and sisters in Christ. From years of coaching and counseling high achievers and senior executives, I've noticed some tendencies that show up all too often.

2 Lutz Group International research of university students—1985 to 1988

1 The high achiever who develops an attitude of reaching his goal at any cost is usually disappointed—even shattered—when he reaches the top of the summit he has been climbing only to realize that a higher mountain has come into view.

2 The individual who dares to look back over the years at the path he has taken, often sees costs that were really too dear when measured against the success.³ Those costs might include divorce, broken health, neglected children, forgotten elderly parents, missed deep friendships, or underdeveloped employees.

3 So-called winners often have a dulled sensitivity to God's ongoing beckoning in their lives.

Remember, if your personal agenda is directed by God's plan for you, He will equip you to navigate the most complex labyrinths you'll ever encounter.

The Apostle Paul demonstrated a remarkable balance between being goal oriented and being adaptive to change. He was a consummate difference maker; a real change agent. Throughout his life, one of his driving goals was to preach the Gospel in Rome and to the political leaders of his day. He would even sacrifice his current good by making troubling decisions to move himself toward Rome. But his entire life perspective was centered on bringing delight to his Lord.

As a result, he was equipped emotionally (heart) and mentally (mind) to thrive on change. And changes came his way again and again in two ways:

1 When God allowed traumatic changes in his life—like wrecking the ship he was sailing to Rome, or throwing him into prison, or leaving him without funds so he had to stop and earn, or causing illness for him or his missionary team, or arranging it so that people wouldn't listen to the Gospel—Paul saw God's hand and searched out the opportunities made possible by the changes.

3 Ordering Your Private World, Gordon MacDonald

2   He was continually checking his spiritual compass through prayer (that effective two-way communication with the Lord). Paul was relentlessly sensing the soul needs and opportunities in the pagan world that surrounded him and making sure he listened to the call and counsel of other Christ-followers near and far.

How does this translate for the student, rising professional, parent, or retiree in today's world? The following RealityCase, "Climbing the Ladder," should add insight and may even cause you to think deeper about your own life.

RealityCase

Climbing the Ladder

My experiences through the years support the saying, I climbed the ladder of success only to find out it was leaning against the wrong building. I had several career changes that weren't on my agenda to prove it.

Back in time, when I was just emerging in my chosen profession as an applied scientist at IBM, I was riding high. I had finished a degree in mathematics at a tough (but small) engineering university four years earlier and was already leading a team on some really critical assignments. Those assignments included NASA, Northwest Airlines, 3M Research, and Mayo Medical Research. I had been fortunate to have a real mentor for a boss who encouraged me to think outside the box and promoted my ideas across the company. I had written several papers on advanced topics that were published (and actually read) in the United States and abroad. Plus, I had been recognized by IBM as one of the top applied scientists in the company.

These kinds of results didn't come easily. I was intensely interested in my work. In fact, I loved it. I thrived on it. I ate it and slept it. My hobby was my work. My relaxation was my work. I had what I now call the fever. And if it hadn't been for my role as a deacon in church and my love for my family, I would have spent every waking moment thinking about work. My manager kept track of my time and quoted to other employees that I had averaged working 70+ hours per week for the last two years and never took my vacation.

The work with NASA was particularly rewarding. Not only did I enjoy solving the challenging problems, it stroked my ego with significant national recognition. In fact, the work became so well known that the head of the Nuclear Accelerator Lab at MIT asked IBM if I could travel to Boston to help solve one of their difficult nuclear accelerator problems. My manager and I jumped at the chance. The contribution was a win-win-win situation—MIT, IBM, and I all succeeded when we got everything figured out.

Then the ultimate next career change presented itself. MIT asked me to consider moving into the Senior Applied Scientist role at MIT. This fit right in with my plan to continually change upwards professionally and personally. I gave the head of the lab a verbal yes, called my wife to share the excitement, and headed home.

Well, when I arrived at the office the next Monday, another change had occurred. Remember that great manager I had? He had been promoted to Chicago and a real turkey (that's what I thought at the time) was in his place. When I told Ev (not his real name), the new manager, about the promotion to the IBM office that handled MIT, he didn't get nearly as glowing and excited as I thought he would. In fact, it was just the opposite. "We'll see about this—and I'll let you know," was all that Ev would say.

Three days later, Ev sent for me. "Tom, you do great work here! After looking at the contacts we have with our big customers in this area and seeing how much they depend on you, I'm going to turn down the promotion for you. In fact, unless I offered it to you, it wouldn't be official anyway." I turned sick with disappointment and was really ticked off with Ev's attitude. "You can't do that! I've worked hard, succeeded for this office, and now you won't let me pursue my life-long ambition!"

"You're young!" he said. "You can't really have too much of a life-long ambition. And besides, the rules in IBM are that the local manager has control over his team—and no one can override my decision. And my decision is that you're too valuable here for me to let you go. Now, if you keep pouring on the coals, and do as well as you have in the past, we'll get you promoted somewhere in a year or so."

"But Ev, the job will be gone by then—and this is the one I've always hoped for and planned on." But Ev would hear nothing of the arguments. His attitude was that he was the boss and he had control. I was crushed as I really began to understand that I didn't control my own future.

I thank God that I was a Christ-follower, and learning to trust Him. Besides, I really enjoyed the work, the customers, and the problems we solved—so I continued to work around the clock.

In the meantime, my wife, Cheke, continued to understand, support, and encourage her workplace superstar. But I wasn't really meeting the needs at home. Cheke hardly ever saw me. I'd leave for work at 6:30 A.M., call her over the noon hour, show up for supper, and then return to the customer until 2 or 3:30 in the morning. I was so thankful for an understanding and patient wife. She was all I could ever ask for—talented, a great mother to our two-year old son, active in Bible Studies and church, and lovely besides. She couldn't have fit better into my plans. Cheke even shared in my dreams and the changes that had come our way, and she would have moved to Boston without a complaint.

Then one night as I came home from a really tough research project with a customer (it was about 2:30 A.M.), I followed my same old routine; milk and cookies in the kitchen, and then quietly sneaking down the unlighted hallway so that I wouldn't wake anyone up. As usual, I planned to undress in the dark and crawl into bed beside my sweet wife without even awakening her. And then it happened! The hall light came on and there stood Cheke—hands on hips and eyes blazing. "Tom, come with me—there is someone I'd like you to meet," she whispered firmly. Had someone come to stay for the night? Was Cheke going to awaken them as she led me down the hall? What was going on?

> Then she moved right past the guest bedroom and motioned for me to follow her into Tommy's room. As she stood over his crib in the dim glow of the Noah's Ark night light, she stated—not whispering—"Here, I'd like you to meet your son! He's been around here for two years, but I'm not sure you've ever met him!" Then she led me back into the lighted hall, looked at me with hurt, disgust, anger, sadness, frustration—all in one expression—stood to the top of her 5'2", 95 pound frame, and said, "Either this neglect of your family stops, or I'm gone—along with Junior."
>
> She literally spit out the next ultimatum. "I don't care what you do for a living as long as it is moral and right—we're going to be a godly and complete family around here. Make your choice. Is it Junior and me (and the baby on the way) or superstar sucker for the IBM corporation?"
>
> Another blow to all the positive, planned, rewarding changes I had envisioned for myself and obviously my family! First my once in a lifetime promotion gets blocked by a turkey manager, and now my wife lays down the "get some balance in your life" ultimatum.

What was the outcome to all of my planned changes? Wisdom? Bitterness? Conforming my will to God's will? Well, it proved to be one more step in building my trust in God and being willing to conform my plans to His will.

NAVIGATION TIP:

Be careful! One of the biggest barriers to change is success.

This is often true for the successful professional. You have set your sights on a worthy and rewarding career. You have studied long and hard in preparing for that career and often proven that you are a master of your profession or trade. Fifteen to twenty years may pass with continuing affirmation of your abilities.

And then it happens! The company is sold, or the plant is closed, or the firm is bought out, or the clients disappear, or the demand for your expertise is no longer needed, or a new boss takes over that has experts of his own, or the work is outsourced, or foreign competition is less expensive and better, or the product is no longer saleable, or . . . And out of nowhere (this is not usually true, but success often creates blindness), you might find yourself out of work. And what if your expertise is no longer needed in the marketplace and you can't find any other company to hire you?

These kinds of changes are not part of anyone's agenda—they are life's plan. The trauma of change in one's professional life is often experienced in several stages. While counseling and coaching executives, I have observed that professional changes often lead to serious shock, denial, bewilderment, self-blame, despondency, depression, and sometimes worse.

The twenty-first century presents a whole new paradigm for thinking about careers and professions. The following table shows the progression to a new way of viewing career changes. Planning for these changes could be a big help for your future.

DECADE	PROGRESSION OF CAREER CHANGE
1970s	Professional climbing, or dealing with boredom, or seeking a change usually meant a change within the company
1980s	The desire to improve oneself or make a change usually caused a person to change companies
1990s	Based on the changes in the culture, marketplace, and compensation, the need for change often meant a change in careers
2000s	One major capability essential in the professional workforce is the ability to make multiple career changes throughout one's work-life

TABLE 5.1

Research in the late 1990s showed that individuals finishing a bachelor's degree and starting in the workforce would be required to change careers (not jobs or companies) at least 3–4 times during their work-life. Our LGI's research updated in 2004 shows that the projection of career changes required of professionals has increased to 5–7 during the 45 years of a person's work-life.

Why? The rate of change is accelerating on almost all of the mind and heart fronts: globalization of markets and workforces, accelerating technology, innovative use of information, diminished soul focus, altered family structures, media and communication technologies, world-wide economies, terrorism, and the list goes on. Want examples? How many buggy whip manufacturers do you know (it was, at one time, a real profession)? To bring it into today's scenario— How secure is the professional chemist who specializes in photographic film manufacture and processing? More than 55% of the cameras purchased today are digital. Kodak reported in October, 2005, that 80% of their revenue in the year 2008 will be from digital.[4]

For the Christ-follower, it's critical to recognize those changes that are signals from the Lord to change course—to modify your agenda. People who are strong-willed find it difficult to give up their agendas.

Here are a few questions designed to help you determine if the Lord wants you to change to a different agenda. The first table (5.2) lists questions and comments for Christ-followers of all ages who are facing significant changes. Then the following tables add issues targeting specific seasons of life—5.3 for young adults, 5.4 for mid-life adults, and 5.5 for seniors (including those who are retired).

Although the questions are stated in a way that requires a yes or no answer, they are really designed to help you think through the decisions and responses for the change maze(s) in front of you. There are no right or wrong answers. The key is that you don't ignore asking yourself the tough questions.

4 USA Today, October 24, 2005

CRITICAL QUESTIONS FOR EVERYONE

	QUESTIONS	COMMENTS
1	Is the potential change consistent with God's Word?	It is important to be in tune with God's will, which is generally clarified in the Scriptures.
2	Has your current agenda provided opportunities for growth and given you joy and delight in the doing?	Don't confuse joy & delight with an easy road to travel. Peace and inner calm are meaningful measurements and might be signals to stay on your current course.
3	Have you earnestly prayed for God to show you how to respond to the change?	The art of listening is critical when carrying on a dialogue with the Lord.
4	Being honest with the Lord and with yourself, do you like the idea of the change?	Sometimes a change becomes a goal in itself and that is often driven by self-interest. Be careful here.
5	Does the change positively impact those around you (family, other Christ-followers, friends, colleagues, etc.)?	Most changes do not affect you alone. If God wants you to change no matter what, He'll take care of those impacted.
6	Are there alternatives to your current agenda and the potential change?	Sometimes the Lord introduces the potential of a change just to get you out of your thinking rut and cause you to tune into Him for your next steps.
7	Have you discussed the potential change with Christ-followers you respect?	God's Word (Proverbs in particular) urges the wise person to seek counsel.
8	Do you feel inadequate to meet the challenge of the change?	Don't be fooled! If God is in the change, you aren't too old or too young, you aren't too poor, you aren't too unprepared, too sick, or too tired to make the change!
9	Are you afraid of the change?	If you are on the Lord's side, there is nothing to fear.
10	Can you clearly see the outcome for you and/or others if the change is made?	God may be putting a change maze in your path to test your faith that He is in control.

TABLE 5.2

ADDITIONAL QUESTIONS FOR YOUNG ADULTS

	QUESTIONS	COMMENTS
Y1	Does this potential change take you away from a Christ-follower value system?	The steps of a righteous man are ordered by the Lord. Be sure to stay on His path.
Y2	Have you looked at the potential benefit of the change several years into the future?	Be careful that you don't make decisions based on the short term view.
Y3	Are you being driven to make this change by pressure from others?	Peer pressure does not necessarily bode well when choosing life's directions.

TABLE 5.3

ADDED QUESTIONS FOR MID-LIFE ADULTS

	QUESTIONS	COMMENTS
M1	Does this change threaten the needs of your family?	Be sure to separate needs from wants.
M2	Does your current agenda offer more opportunity to grow spiritually than the potential change?	Eternal values should override the mind and heart.
M3	With your growing responsibilities, are you becoming risk averse?	Many opportunities are missed because a person fails to rely on the Lord when called by Him to do new things.

TABLE 5.4

ADDED QUESTIONS FOR SENIOR ADULTS

	QUESTIONS	COMMENTS
S1	Do you think you have earned the right to be comfortable in your current agenda?	God didn't move Moses into his position of leadership until he was in his 80s.
S2	Are you using the excuse that you can't accept new changes because your current agenda is for the kids and grandkids?	God will guide them into His will just like He may be guiding you to do new things for Him.
S3	Are you open to the Lord using this change in your life as a way to take advantage of all the experiences and benefits He's given you?	Make sure you listen to Him, not your family, not your buddies, not your tired body.
S4	Are you following your agenda to retire when God has given you health, resources, and challenges to serve Him?	Where is retirement described in the scriptures?
S5	What are the primary objectives of your last will and testament?	Evaluate your plans for after you're gone in the light of Him over your family.

TABLE 5.5

If you are goal oriented and striving for success, dealing with change that challenges your agenda is tough and the experience can be dysfunctional. To begin to plan your approach to a change maze in front of you, ask yourself these questions:

1 How does the change fit into my agenda?

2 Am I so set on my agenda that I will only be satisfied if the change can be adjusted to conform to me?

3 How would this change impact my goal of being Christ-Centered?

4 Does this change lead me to change my agenda?

It is this last question that should open your mind to seek God's (re)direction for future plans and the possibility of a new agenda.

Section 2 Chapter 5 PonderPoints

1. The following graph shows two of the culture changes that are currently in effect in the United States. The Christian Culture is moving into the decay stage and the Humanist Culture is in the growth stage.

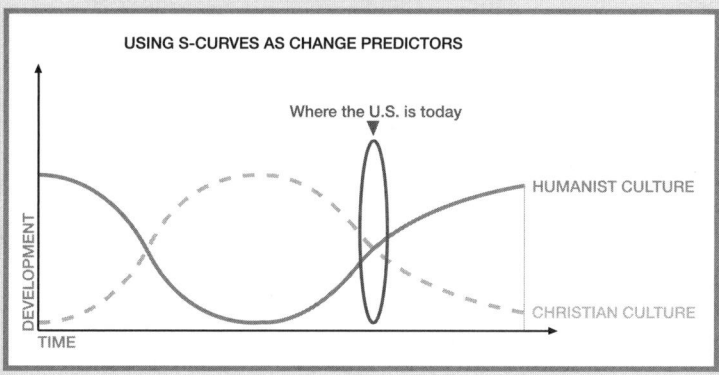

In order to deal with these complex changes that are shown in the graph, list a few changes that you could plan for your life that might reverse or at least slow down their impact on you. Indicate whether the planned changes are primarily concerned with facts (mind), emotions (heart), or faith (soul) changes.

SUGGESTED PLAN CHANGE	PRIMARY DIMENSION
1	__Mind __Heart __Soul
2	__Mind __Heart __Soul

2. If you have a last will and testament, look at it carefully and determine what's written into it. It is, after all, a plan to deal with the predictable change of your death. Construct a table with Mind, Heart, and Soul as columns. Then go through it and list under the appropriate heading each of the items in your will. Finally, go back to the Scripture (Luke 12:16-20) and ask yourself how you think your plan measures up in God's eyes.

CHAPTER SIX

Navigating Unpredictable Changes:
Sporadic and Blind-Side

Have you ever been awakened by a ringing phone in the night to find out that a friend or relative has been in a wreck? Did you ever get a call from your kid's teacher saying that your child was about to flunk a course in which you thought he was doing well? Have you been on your 25th anniversary trip and found out when you called to check on the kids that one of your sons has been arrested for swimming in the city reservoir? (That actually happened to Cheke and me!)

The previous three chapters addressed predictable change and examined ways to plan for them. Now we're going to move on to more difficult changes. Think of it this way. Until now we have been confronting change mazes that were more like those we solve by looking at them on a piece of paper: two-dimensional and viewed from above. We can sometimes look ahead (because the change is predictable) and figure out what might happen if we choose one turn or another.

FIGURE 6.1

Now we're beginning to face mazes that are three-dimensional—the corridors have walls and they aren't simple mazes anymore. They are labyrinths with walls we can't see over.

> labyrinth (n): a — a place constructed of or full of intricate passageways and blind alleys; b – a maze (as in a garden) formed by paths separated by high hedges; c — something extremely complex or tortuous in structure, arrangement, or character.[5]

FIGURE 6.2

5 *Merriam-Webster's Collegiate Dictionary—Eleventh Edition*

In the case of unpredictable change, you are thrust into the labyrinth without warning and given no option to change or not change. You feel like Dorothy in the Wizard of Oz when she was picked up from the plains of Kansas and plopped into the Land of Oz. Or like the surfer who is enjoying the ride, not realizing that he is about to be swamped by a huge wave.

  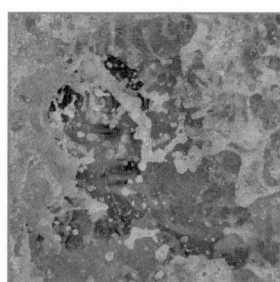

Before I give you some principles to help you work your way through and out of the labyrinth, let's identify some of the characteristics of these kinds of changes that will help you orient your compass and get your bearings.

These change labyrinths come in ways and times that are not expected. Two examples come to mind. The first is the day when Christ will return to establish His eternal kingdom. The scripture says that "the day of the Lord will come just like a thief in the night" I Thessalonians 5:2.

The second is one we've observed in the United States: terrorist attacks. Notice I said "attacks." We usually focus on the terrible tragedy that happened on 9-11-2001. But a quick study of attacks on United States' interests around the world shows us that there have been more than seventy in the last five years.

Do you agree that both Christ's second coming and terrorist attacks have caused or will cause tremendous, traumatic, life-changing change? They were and are predictable. But in terms of how we manage ourselves when they hit, it is helpful to view them as unpredictable. Here are some of the characteristics that are important to note:

- The change blindsides you. You don't know where it came from, you don't seem to have any option to reject the change, and you can't ignore it.

- The frequency of the change is sporadic. The arrival time of the change is unpredictable. And in many cases, it or something like it comes more than once. An example is the tragic Hurricane Katrina that inundated the southern coast of the United States and was followed a few weeks later by Hurricane Rita and then a month later by Hurricane Wilma. The barometric pressures were lower than any on record, and the number of hurricanes in a season was another record.

- The change hits quickly. And once you're in the labyrinth, it seems to accelerate.

- The magnitude of the change appears to be big. (That isn't always the case, but because it catches you by surprise, you see it as major.)

- Most people initially react to the change by moving to the resistance side of the Change Capacity Spectrum.

- If a person has had previous successes when facing similar changes, the tendency is to ignore or downplay the potential outcomes. (People in New Orleans had survived previous hurricanes so when they were told to evacuate because Katrina was coming, many failed to respond. Some lost their lives as a result.)

Blind-sided and sporadic changes are those that sap a person's energy, cause sleepless nights, and blur other important issues in life. Such changes are so sudden, so unpredictable, so traumatic, so far reaching (at least to you), that you almost become dysfunctional.

There are several examples of blind-sided and sporadic change that are familiar to most people in the United States. (Note: Some of the changes were not blind-sided at all—they were, in fact, predictable. But to people who chose to ignore the change maze in front of them, it blind-sided them.)

1 The desegregation of schools in the U.S. in the 1960s

2 The banning of prayer in schools in the U.S.

3 The terrorists attacks on the World Trade Center in New York and the Pentagon in Washington D.C. on 9/11/2001

4 The tsunami that hit the South Pacific in 2004

5 The outbreak of HIV across the world

You may consider some of these changes to be positive and others negative. That's not the point. The issue here is that first of all, they changed the culture, structure, and life of most citizens of the United States. Secondly, some of these examples can be extremely complex. Our minds are filled with facts (both pro and con) relating to the past, the change itself, and the ongoing impact. Even more critical is that our hearts (emotions) get enmeshed with these changes. Facts can become distorted in such a way that denial, bitterness, hostility, futility, excitement, anticipation, optimism, and delight all begin to play a part in a our inability to function rationally.

Let's get closer to home with some examples of blind-side changes that you may be able to relate to personally or at least imagine realistically.

1 The price of gasoline skyrocketed in 6 months

2 Your beloved senior pastor at church suddenly resigned

3 A clean-cut close friend (or family member) was arrested for drug possession

4 Your parents suddenly announced they were getting a divorce

5 The bank called to tell you that your account was overdrawn

6 Your teacher announced to the class that your term paper was the best she ever read

7 The doctors just told you that your 6', 180 pound, seemingly healthy son has a cancerous tumor

8 The company you worked for was just sold and you were released because your position was redundant

Can you add to the list? Some of these examples aren't too serious and others are life changing. The key is that they came when they weren't expected. Some of them placed you right into the middle of a change labyrinth with no directions on how to get out. So what do you do? How do you operate under those conditions?

One of the tendencies humans beings have when surprised with a sporadic and blind-sided change is to forget who you are and how you normally operate along the Change Capacities Spectrum (Figure 6.4). Since sporadic change comes on the scene by surprise and blind-sides you, you usually don't know a lot about it. The natural tendency is to hunker down and become a resistor. You long for the status-quo even though that may not be the best for you. You will probably be pushed to the left of the curve even if that isn't where you function the best.

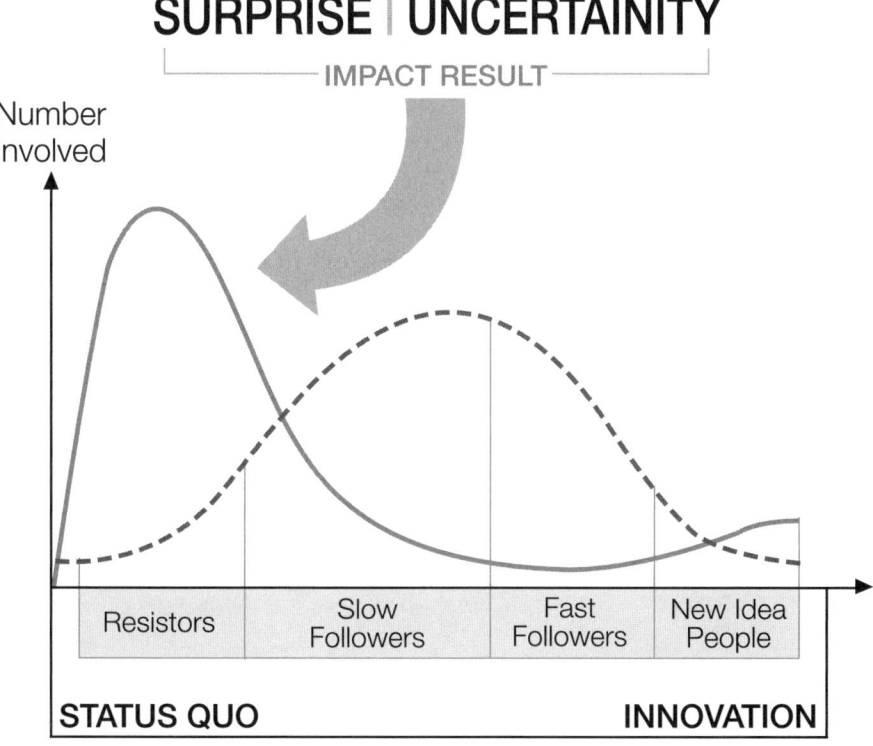

FIGURE 6.4

As a pilot, my instructors taught me critical procedures and then hammered on the fact that they must be followed. More than once, my life (and the airplane) was spared because it became routine for me to remember and follow the steps. I recall one incident in particular. It was a fall day, clear and quiet, and

I was returning home from a speaking engagement in Iowa. The single engine Bonanza was moving right along and autopilot was keeping me on course. It was a great opportunity to enjoy the landscape.

And then the engine quit. It really got quiet. My first impulse was to panic; a sporadic blind-side change was happening. Then I remembered what I had been taught. The first step is to take control of the plane and get it set up for the longest possible glide. Step two was to look for a place to land, even if it was a highway or open field. I did all of that almost automatically. The next step was to check the fuel gauges and the indicator of which fuel tank I was using. Sure enough, I had forgotten to switch tanks an hour earlier and had run the left tank dry. A simple flip of a switch and the engine came to life as it got the fuel it needed. The whole incident took about 2 minutes, but I was sweating. The procedure had turned a traumatic change into something far less threatening. In the same way, you can develop an effective check list that could help you navigate your way through sporadic blind-side changes. Here is a summary of mine.

BLIND-SIDE ✔LIST

✔		ACTION
	1	Get on your knees and ask God to calm you. Don't follow your emotions to run in panic.
	2	Concentrate on where you are in the labyrinth. Don't focus on how you got there.
	3	Stop and reflect. Is it the change that is causing your trauma or is it the fact that you were surprised? (When you calm down, you may see the labyrinth shrink because the change isn't such a big deal.)
	4	Look back over your experiences. Have you ever been faced with a change like this before? If so, can you remember what you did then? That experience can guide you to what you should or shouldn't do to navigate now.
	5	Call a Christ-follower friend. One you can trust to be objective and confidential. Take the time to describe the change. Ask the friend to help you distinguish between the mind and heart dimensions. Talk it through. He probably won't be able to navigate for you, but it should help clean your windshield of extraneous bugs so you can see the labyrinth corridors more clearly.
	6	Look at yourself in the Change Capacity mirror. Determine whether you've allowed the change to shove you into territory where you don't normally operate. If it has, get back to where you function the best.

Section 2 Chapter 6 PonderPoints

1. Identify a change that surprised you or your family recently. (Try to recall a change that is more significant than the hamburger burned on the grill.) By working your way through the following questions, you can practice the simple check list given at the end of the chapter.

   a. In a few sentences, describe the change and how it presented itself. Try to be as objective and factual as you can.

   b. What were your emotions when you first realized it had blind-sided you?

   c. Honestly, before you reacted, did you have time or take time to pray about the situation?

   d. On the Change Capacity graph, where do you think you are?

NORMALLY	**WHEN THE CHANGE HIT**
___ Resistor	___ Resistor
___ Slow Follower	___ Slow Follower
___ Fast Follower	___ Fast Follower
___ New Idea Person	___ New Idea Person

e. Were you able to separate the facts of the change from your emotions about it? Complete the following table.

FACTS	EMOTIONS

f. Have you discussed the issues surrounding the blind-side change with a confidant? Did articulating the facts help you build a plan to navigate in the labyrinth? If so, how?

g. Are you still in the maze? Do you think you'll ever emerge from it? If not, how will living in the labyrinth impact your life? Can you live with it? Consider Psalm 46:1: "God is our refuge and strength, a very present help in trouble."

CHAPTER SEVEN
Managing the Trauma
of Blind-Side Changes: Hitting the Wall

What if you've been dropped into the middle of a change labyrinth? What if you don't know which way to turn, and there is nothing but a wall in front of you, and you aren't thinking too clearly? Later in this chapter I'll describe what happened when our son, Tim, felt he was in that kind of maze. He hit the wall.

In chapter two we discussed the change shapers: magnitude, risk and uncertainty, rate of change, and success. Most of them show up when you're blind-sided by change. Have you been blind-sided by change lately? Was the change so traumatic that you lost your cool or you went into a frump or you were beside yourself (whatever that means)?

Let's look more closely at the shaper called magnitude to see how it creates the trauma that often accompanies blind-side changes. The magnitude of change has three components:

VOLUME (number of changes per unit time)

MOMENTUM (time it takes for the change to play out)

COMPLEXITY (number of components within each change)

Figure 7.1 illustrates the case where the magnitude of change is continually increasing. At the same time, you have your own resilience for change. Some have low resilience and others have high resilience. The dysfunctional wall is defined as the point where the magnitude of change and the resilience for change collide! As more changes load up on a person, resilience shifts to resistance, even when you originally wanted to change.

WHEN A PERSON "HITS THE WALL"

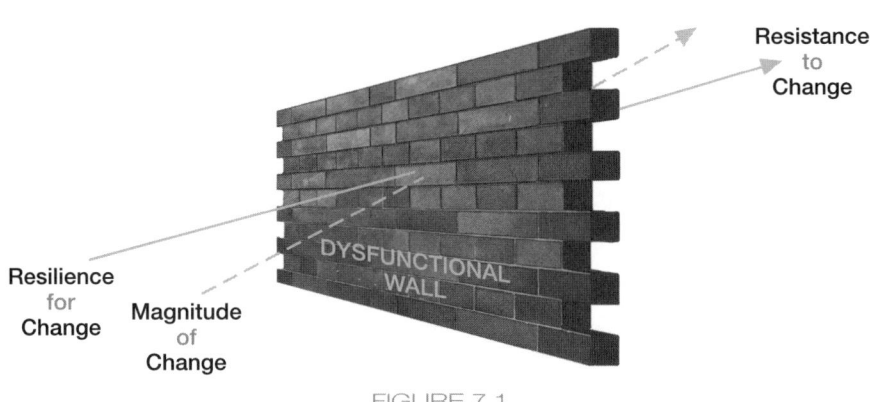

FIGURE 7.1

Many characteristics define how and when different individuals hit the wall; for instance, age, emotional strength, toughness, stamina, fatigue, family and friend support, optimism, self-worth, and family stability. One characteristic ranks above others, however, in your ability to be resilient in the time of change—your spiritual (soul) strength.

In the twenty-first century, the rate of change continues to accelerate, and we find ourselves at the dysfunctional wall sooner than ever. More changes, coming faster, with increased complexity and more sporadically, can push you beyond your ability to handle the changes. Almost everyone has a breaking point, with a variety of possible results. Some or all of the following may occur.

	SIGNS OF HITTING THE WALL	INDICATIVE RESPONSES
1	Denial	Ignore the change
2	Lack of understanding	Avoid getting the facts
3	Frustration	Plead confusion
4	Anxiety	Be upset and lose sleep
5	Anger & Hostility	Display hostile behavior
6	Declaration that change is unacceptable	Attempt to undo the change
7	Irrational thinking (Heart takes over the Mind)	Become irrational (falsify the facts, make accusations, take steps designed to take things back to before the change, organize resistance, introduce counter-changes)
8	Sadness & self pity	Withdraw
9	Grief	Fail to function properly, remain silent or over communicate
10	Depression	Withdraw further and/or attack others
11	Unrelenting depression	Attempt suicide and/or other violent venting

TABLE 7.2

There are several principles that you can apply when change mazes begin to look like a dysfunctional wall.

PRINCIPLE 1

Keep the number of changes to a critical few. Most people try to adapt and respond to far too many demands. Every new pressure seems critical, and often it is, but you can only juggle so many changes at a time. Here are some ways to do this.

a. Identify the actual critical changes that need to be addressed. List them; separate the real pending changes from those that are not so real.

b. Pray about which changes the Lord wants you to tackle, and ask Him how.

c. Prioritize the real ones from high to low, and then pick the top few to work through; set the rest aside.

d. Once one is "handled," add another to the list from those set aside earlier. (Note: Often some changes that seemed inevitable and critical but which you have not had time to deal with will disappear or become inconsequential as time passes.)

e. Update the list with new changes that have appeared, drop those that have been dealt with, and drop the ones that have actually disappeared (don't keep resurrecting those that have passed).

f. Be careful that you don't try to boil the ocean.

PRINCIPLE 2

If you can't control the number of changes, move the dysfunctional wall. Begin by trying to determine your capacity for change. God has given some individuals the ability to deal with many changes and issues at the same time while others of us have the skills to handle only a few. An honest appraisal by others who are close to you can help you determine your threshold of chaos. Then apply Principle 1 to pick off the most critical changes one at a time. Order moves a person's dysfunctional wall to the right; chaos moves it to the left.

Understand why the wall is where it is, and try to remove those frustrations that overwhelm you. Know your limits and don't accept ownership of more than you can handle. This takes discipline and a concentrated focus on what the Lord wants you to handle. Emphasis on your soul through prayer, absorbing the Scriptures, and fellowship with other Christ-Followers will bring contentment, a clearer mind, and a Christ-Centered heart.

Note in Figure 7.3 that the dysfunctional wall moves to the right as a person's resilience for change improves. Also compare Figures 7.1 and 7.3. The magnitude of change doesn't let up. The point is that you can't control the rate or the magnitude of the change that comes your way. But you can control how you respond to those changes.

Recognize, too, that moving the wall takes concentrated attention. It is similar to building muscles; you must develop a plan to build strength, and then follow that plan by adding a bit more exercise (and slightly heavier weights) on a regular basis. A juggler does not learn to juggle 7–10 balls by starting with that many. Usually he starts with two. Then, after managing that well, he adds another. And then another. Finally he is able to reach his goal. In combination with Principle 1, recognize that the best way to frustrate a juggler is to toss another ball into the mix as he is juggling at his maximum. Chances are, he will drop all of them. That is like hitting his dysfunctional wall.

TO COPE WITH THE RATE OF CHANGE, MOVE THE WALL

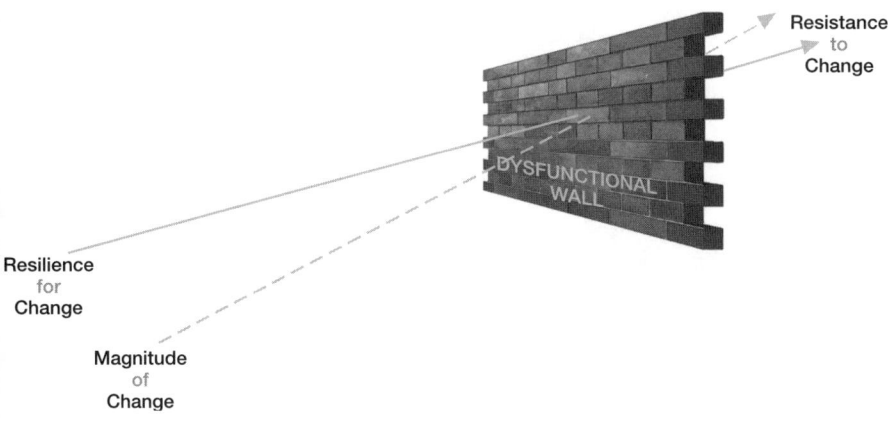

FIGURE 7.3

PRINCIPLE 3

Build relationships with a team of resilient people. The best place to find these resilient people is among Christ-followers (and that should be in the church). The reason? Christ-followers are focused on eternity, which gives them a resiliency that keeps change in perspective.

In a Christ-follower team, the more resilient people will help improve the less resilient ones. Seek out people who are unflappable in the face of adversity and change.

PRINCIPLE 4

Build a stable foundation of nonnegotiable beliefs based on Christ and His Word. People who successfully handle all kinds of changes well have firm basic beliefs and defined values, and live them. Individuals who have solid faith, with well-stated absolutes and meaningful moral and ethical standards, will have a strong foundation for resiliency. Under the pressure of war, the enemy often tries to break its prisoners by overwhelming them with terrible conditions, continual uncertainty, and constant, traumatic, sporadic changes. Prisoners who have a strong faith and strong roots in absolutes are by far the most resilient under devastating conditions.

Let's look at some examples. The first is a famous blind-sided change case right out of the Bible.

> Then Satan answered the Lord, "Does Job fear God for nothing? Have you made a hedge about him and his house and all that he has, on every side? You have blessed the work of his hands and his possessions have increased in the land. But put forth Your hand now and touch all that he has; he will surely curse You to Your face."

> Then the Lord said to Satan, "Behold, all that he has is in your power, only do not put forth your hand on him." So Satan departed from the presence of the Lord.
>
> Job 1:9–12

Poor Job! He had no idea that he would be the target of all that Satan could throw at him. In one of the most famous books about suffering in all of literature, this great man of God was blind-sided with unpredictable, traumatic, sporadic, accelerated, complex, bewildering, intensified change.

These are the kind of changes that break people. As a result of such changes, a person is often referred to as never being the same again. And in many cases, these kind of changes cause people to give up. When the mind is presented with so many radical facts, suddenly, the heart (emotions) can't handle them.

The following RealityCase describes the blind-side changes, the dysfunctional wall, and the tragic outcome of low resilience in the face of change.

Running Out of Cope

Our son, Tim, was finally getting a grip on his future. Since his first or second year of college, life had not been the way he or Cheke and I had hoped. Oh, don't worry. He had had plenty of fun while in school and then on his own. But it sure wasn't lasting fun, and he knew the difference.

During his senior year of college, he had cast about for jobs. The kind of job he wanted, something in real estate development, would have used his uncanny eye for land values and applied his intuitive ability to visualize creative designs for both residential and commercial development. Besides, he had a persuasive personality that caused almost everyone to trust his ideas and enjoy his company.

The only problem was, he had majored in finance (for a reason no one will understand to this day) and really did poorly. In fact, he graduated with the absolute minimum accomplishments while still qualifying for a degree in four years. (He had always said he would outdo his older brother—he'd finish in exactly four years.) The result was that no one would hire him in his field of interest.

After graduation, he settled in for rest and relaxation while living at home. Well, after a few months, I introduced uncomfortable change for Tim. "This isn't getting you anywhere, so it's time you get out on your own. You proved you could do it when you worked while in school, so plan to be gone in a few weeks." After a few heated arguments, Tim understood. (I think he knew all along that we really loved him—and that part of growing up was building his future on his own.) With tears all around, Tim left for the east coast (Connecticut to be exact) where we had lived for several years while he was in his early teens. He had enough money in his pocket to survive for three months if he was careful and he had a good car (plus his prized stereo packed along with a good assortment of clothes—compliments of Mom).

The next three years in the East weren't easy. He became the director of marketing for a small, but highly successful family-owned business. And Tim did well, position-wise. But he really didn't get along with the heir to the ownership (the founder's son) whom Tim considered lazy and ineffective as director of operations. And Tim wasn't hesitant to speak his mind. His company kept him because he did a fine job, but neither his employer nor Tim was happy about it. And Tim didn't really like the work. He still longed for a job where he believed he had the talents but he just didn't have the credentials.

Although he did well financially, his spending habits outstripped his income. Sound familiar for a 24-year old? As his unhappiness grew and his creditors began to hound him, he finally admitted his failings and turned to us. After careful consideration, I relented. "Come home, work for me in marketing (although it isn't your first love), pay off your bills, and search for the right job while under our care and guidance. And by the way, you can begin to get yourself in touch with the

Lord again!"

Well, Tim saw this as a chance for a whole new start. In fact, he really decided to build a new beginning. He even changed his name officially to Tanner Dakota West. And he started to go to church on a regular basis (at least to satisfy Cheke and me).

The work went well. Besides a reasonable salary, the bonuses were good and often. He really did know how to sell my services, and he was an excellent salesman. By living at home in an apartment in the lower level, he saved money. And he paid off his debts.

But he still wasn't doing what he wanted to do. And he knew the job with me was only temporary. So he continued to search for the dream, real estate development. After months of sending out résumés, going through personal and telephone interviews, he got the offer he had always dreamed of. He was hired to be the project manager of a small patio home development; and it was in North Carolina, the state where he had gone to college. He loved the thought of it. And the job even included a new pickup truck so he wouldn't have to buy a vehicle. God had really made the waiting worthwhile, and Tim/Tanner was oh, so thankful.

Before leaving us for the second time, he called his new employer. "Should I buy my new pickup here? I found a good deal on the one I'd like. What do you think?" After a long pause, the new boss (Stan) said, "You better wait until you get here and then we'll look for it together. Maybe we won't get a new one; just one that will get you by and keep the project costs down."

Well, Tim never did like waiting so he put the arm on me for a loan. He'd combine whatever Stan planned to spend with his new income to pay me back. "No, son. You still have trouble with patience so I won't loan you the money." That almost made the second parting a crisis, but finally, with lots of love, hugs, tears, and prayer, Tim left for his new job.

Then the roof fell in; or at least Tim's dream turned into a nightmare. When he got to North Carolina, the job evaporated. Stan wouldn't even meet with him. It seems that Stan, and the project, were in serious financial difficulties and headed for bankruptcy. He didn't have the money to pay Tim, let alone provide him with a truck. Tim/Tanner had been blindsided again. Yes, looking back, he thought something was funny when he tried to go ahead with getting a truck, but his hopes had been so high, he just didn't see the signs.

Well, matters got worse. With little money, he went from part-time job to part-time job; cleaning stables, scrubbing boats, waiting tables. He talked a landowner with a condemned house into letting him live in it. For Christmas he only asked us for a gas grill with a side burner. He wheeled it into the old run-down kitchen and used it for a stove. He got the pump working from the well so he had running water but the only way it got warm was on the burner of his grill. He got some old lumber to board up the cracks, got his hands on a second-hand wood stove for heat, and really made it quite homey.

Then he met Holly. She was so sweet—and really gave him some ambition again. Tim remembered what he had been taught and knew what God wanted of him in terms of dating, and he honored his Lord. As for Holly, she really respected him for it. Their relationship grew, and they began to talk of marriage.

But there just wasn't any good work in North Carolina for Tim/Tanner. So, for the third time, he headed back home–again to work for me. Holly stayed in North Carolina but there was lots of travel—in both directions. As before, Tim was successful.

Now he began to think of a house for them—Holly and him. He put his real estate skills to work and found a great piece of land with an old house and barn on 11 acres in the hills and only 15 minutes from work. He had visions of developing 10 acres—selling them as separate lots—and living in the old house and fixing up the barn for a real estate development business. And the price was right. He had no debt and he made enough working for me to make the payments. The bank (who owned the land) wanted to move it and required almost no down payment.

Then Tanner got blindsided again. His past, as Tim, followed him. He may have changed his name and paid his debts, but credit ratings stick with the person's Social Security number, and that doesn't change when you change your name! The bank gave an almost impolite "no" to his loan application.

Tanner, or Tim, was despondent to say the least. And he had been troubled with depression since his third year of college. "Dad, I'm going to see a psychiatrist. Is it okay if I'm out of the office for a couple of hours? I can't even sleep at night. In fact, you better hide your shotgun or I might do something with it." With that, he headed down the driveway—hoping for some help.

While Tanner was gone, a phone call from North Carolina came into the office. "I'd like to speak with Tanner." My reply was, "He's not here and will be back in a few hours."

"Well then, give him this message. I understand that he keeps calling my girlfriend, Holly, and I want him to knock it off." My stunned reply was, "Call him back in a few hours and tell him yourself. I'm not going to get into the middle of this."

When Tim got back, I told him about the message in hopes that it would prepare him for the call. (I regret doing that to this day.) "Is that what the guy really said? I didn't even know she had anyone but me!" As his face turned gray, he began to pace. "Dad, I finally got some medicine to help with my depression, but it won't really be effective for about 15 days. With Holly dating some other guy, and all that's happened, I don't think I can wait that long."

Several hours later, after Cheke and I returned from showing foreign friends around town, we found a note on the garage door. In effect it said, "It was nobody's fault! Here are the phone numbers of three people to call. (And it listed the names and numbers.)"

I tried to keep Cheke from going in, but she wouldn't stay back. We found Tim's body on his bed—having taken his own life. On the night-stand was a tape recorder with a message.

"There were so many changes—so many things that were against me—I just lost hope. I tried to call my closest friend, Bill, and he was gone. I tried to call Holly, and she wasn't there. Dad, I believe that Christ saved me, but my faith is different than yours. I know I'll be in heaven when this is over, but He doesn't really involve Himself in my

> life now! I know because I prayed for help for years and He just didn't listen. This is no one's fault. But now I won't be a burden to you, to Holly, to our family—and I'll be at peace. I just don't have any more hope left in me. I love you. Thanks for everything!   –Tim"

In the above RealityCase, hindsight shows several points where we should have taken action to help Tim avoid the wall; but we didn't. Many questions about the suicide surface in our minds to this day. The ricochet of someone hitting the wall can be major and unavoidable. It impacts family, church family, friends, work associates, and even the community—but most of all, it can impact a person's relationship with Christ. (Cheke and I thank God that it did impact us for good; giving us a deeper grasp of His Love and His sovereignty. He has even encouraged me to write a book about the subject. You're reading it!) We didn't heed Job's wife's advice: *"Do you still hold fast to your integrity? Curse God and die!"* Job 2:9

When a disastrous change hits and the person uses only facts and emotions to deal with it, the likelihood of becoming dysfunctional increases significantly. Look at the progression of steps toward hitting the wall.

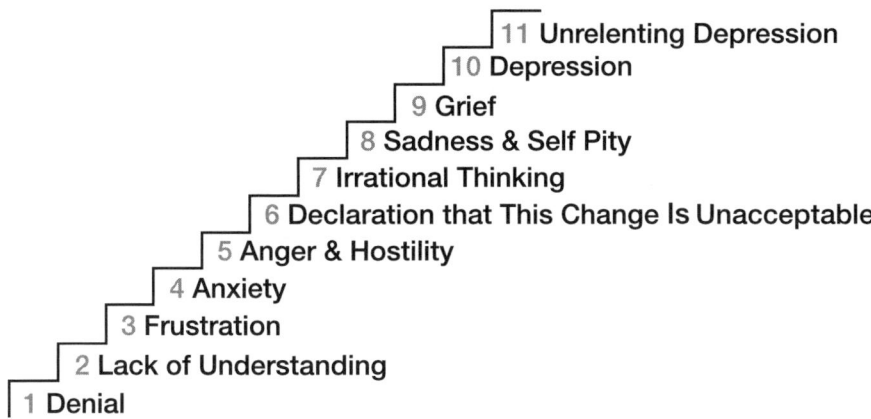

FIGURE 7.4

Usually a blind-side change that sends a person headlong toward the dysfunctional wall is the kind of change that can't be avoided or reversed—a sudden death of someone close, an unexpected loss of a job (and no new employment in sight), a stock market crash, or a natural disaster (hurricane, tornado, fire, flood), for example. It is such a dramatic change that dysfunction is expected and might even be considered normal by some.

My experiences while teaching and consulting aren't all pretty, as the following examples show: The young father who woke up one morning to find that his wife had died unexpectedly during the night and who has been sitting in his home grieving, neglecting his young daughters of four and seven, has crashed into the wall. The successful business man who is suddenly let go and refuses to tell his wife and pretends to go to work for months by going to the library has crashed into the wall. A loving sister who loses her home to a tornado that wiped out their development and then won't communicate with a sibling for years has crashed into the wall.

Section 2 Chapter 7 PonderPoints

1. Have you (or someone you know) ever been so blind-sided by a change that you became dysfunctional? Here are a few questions to ponder as you look back.

   a. Briefly describe the blind-side change.

   b. What made it blind-side?

   c. What was your initial reaction when it hit?

   d. Did you move up the dysfunction steps? How far?

   e. Did you stay on that step? Are you still caught in the change labyrinth?

   f. How did your response and actions impact people around you?

   g. What have you done to get back to normal?

   h. What could you have done better to reduce the impact of hitting the wall?

i. How has the blind-side change shaped your life?

j. How has the impact of hitting the wall shaped your view of eternity and your relationship with Christ?

2. Do you know anyone who has had blind-side change after change after change but has not hit the dysfunctional wall?

a. What has helped that person push the wall away to gain a greater tolerance for change?

b. Read Job 2:10 for Job's reply to his wife. (Remember this is after Job was blind-sided by a number of tragic changes.) How do you explain his refusal to crash into the wall?

CHAPTER EIGHT
Reducing the Impact
When Walls Are Inevitable

Sometimes the Lord calms the storm,
Sometimes He lets the storm rage and calms His child.
Anonymous

Not all traumatic blind-side changes cause a person to go through every step from Denial to Unrelenting Depression. Depending on your emotional state, maturity, physical well-being, and ability to remain calm in the face of difficulty, you may or may not find it easy to recognize what's happening and take action. The good news is, you can reduce the impact of hitting the wall. Here are two shock absorbers:

1 Move the Wall

2 Find Peace in the Change

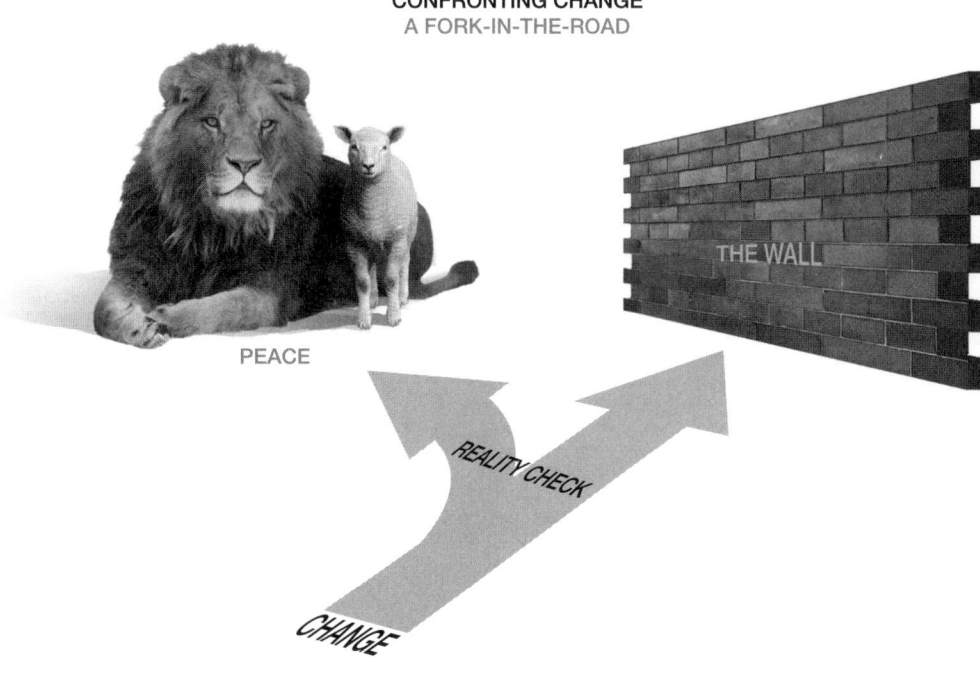

FIGURE 8.1

As discussed in Chapter 7, moving the wall means pushing it away by increasing your resilience. But what can you do now to move a dysfunctional wall? What actions can you take to enhance your ability to cope; especially with traumatic blind-side change? Here are a few actions that could help push dysfunctional walls out of your life in the years ahead.

ACTIONS	EXPLANATION
Build a 1-on-1 relationship with God	Recognize that you are a child of God and have access to Him. Begin each day by communicating with Him in prayer and Bible study. Talk with God continually throughout the day; listen and watch for His direction as you face changes you can't handle or understand.
View everything as an issue of faith.	As you move from being hung up on you (self-centered) to being sold out to Him (Christ-centered), the facts of the mind and the emotions of your heart will take on an eternal perspective. You'll be amazed at how crises will become less troublesome.
Become part of a Christ-centered church	Find a church that is centered on Christ, faithful to God's Word (the Bible), has a heart that serves others, reaches out to the unlovely, and has real joy and excitement being together. Then become a part of it! And that means becoming involved in worshipping, serving, reaching, and growing in your relationship with Him.
Develop a core of godly real friends	There are friends—and there are real friends. And as a Christ-follower, you should surround yourself with Christ-follower friends who love you and whom you love, people whom you can be honest and vulnerable with, and who will be there when the troubling changes hit.
Find valued professional help when faced with "the wall"	Some changes that impact us are well beyond our ability to grasp. And yet they must be met directly. There are professionals—counselors, pastors, psychologists—that can help you identify where you are on the steps/signs toward the dysfunctional wall and coach you to move the wall. But be careful. Make sure that this "help" understands and is involved with the Lord that you follow.
Reflect on where you are on the "Signs of Hitting the Wall"	Take the time to match your reaction to change to the signs that show you where you are as you approach the wall. Often, just the realization of how you have responded to a change so far will help you get off the path to more exasperation than you can handle.
Ignore those changes that you can't control	Above all, even though you may abhor and want to resist a certain change, evaluate whether you have any control whatsoever over the change. And if not, ignore it. (Note: That doesn't mean don't pray about it and ask the Lord to work a miracle—but let go and move onto those issues in your life that you can impact.)

TABLE 8.2

Sometimes moving the wall takes a long time. And it often means that someone else must intervene to get you on the right track. Pete, in the following RealityCase, was unable to "make it happen" on his own.

 RealityCase

God's Specialty: Moving the Wall

At 5:30 A.M. I finally made the tough decision. I had tossed and turned since coming to bed at midnight, and there had been no sleep all night. I had to release—fire—Pete Johannson! There was no alternative. I had tried everything I knew and it hadn't worked.

A recap of the history: I had personally recruited Pete to be one of my five key directors two years earlier. He had a superb background, and for the first seven or eight months proved to be the right choice. Pete was a sound manager, made excellent executive decisions, led his people well, and really pleased our company's clients. What more could the company want?

Then Pete began to miss appointments . . . and mess up assignments . . . and misuse his people . . . and insult clients . . . and forget to show up at work. No, it didn't happen all at once. It got progressively worse over a six-month stretch to the point that the other directors had to cover for Pete's slippage.

We tried everything. We started by trying to encourage Pete to adjust his personal administrative style. Then, after that didn't work, we tried to motivate Pete with a special bonus program. And finally, I gave Pete the low evaluation he deserved. Oh, Pete was contrite and pledged to do better, but that only lasted for a few weeks.

One evening I stopped by the office and saw Pete's office light on. As I knocked on his door, I heard strange sounds but not the familiar "It's open—come on in." After waiting a bit, I slowly opened the door to find Pete slumped, or slouched, or sprawled, or . . . in his chair with his head back and his eyes unfocused. It didn't take a doctor to quickly sort out that Pete was very intoxicated. The empty bottle on his desk and the spilled liquid all over everything confirmed it. Pete was totally incoherent and unable to talk, walk, or even lift his head. I called the company medics and they quickly arranged for an ambulance to take Pete to a well-run "detox" unit to sober up.

Three days later Pete and I had one of those Dutch uncle talks. Pete was more than contrite and terribly embarrassed by his behavior. He pledged to do better and claimed that this was not a common occurrence. And for about a month, Pete was again his model self. Then he began to slip back into his old habits—missing appointments . . . and messing up assignments . . . and misusing his people . . . and insulting clients . . . and forgetting to show up for work.

But this time I knew what to address and how to deal with it. "Pete, either you agree to an alcohol treatment and rehabilitation program or I'm going to have to let you go." But this time Pete was in denial and had some feasible excuses. "You know that I've been going through a terrible divorce. After my wife tried to kill me, I've still had lengthy court fights to get custody of the kids and that's been so emotionally tough. Now that we're almost through that, I'll not drink anymore. Alcohol has just been an escape and I guess I got carried away. But I can stop anytime and I'll commit to stop now."

With that promise, we agreed to forego the treatment program. And Pete again became the model director (for about four months this time). Then the problems hit again. This time I got tough. "Pete, either it's treatment and rehabilitation, or you're gone." Pete knew he couldn't argue, so he signed the papers, got someone to look after the kids (ages 14, 11, and 4) and checked in to a 30-day program.

A month later Pete was back, looking good, and ready to work. "Tom, you don't know how much I owe you for sticking with me and getting me to admit my alcohol problem. That was the worst/best 30 days of my life." "Well, Pete, the Scriptures have taught me a lot about management. They indicate that the first thing to do when finding someone doing something that they shouldn't do is to make every effort to restore them. We want you whole and productive and proud of your work. I'm glad it did the job. Also know that in our Bible Study group, we've been praying for you and your family. Thank God for His help."

Everything worked well for about six months. Then one day, Pete didn't even show up for work and no one could reach him at home.

The company CEO got involved and acknowledged that the company and I had done everything that could be done and it was now my responsibility to take the next step. He would back any action I would take, but something had to be done.

Those were the facts that were rolling around in my head as I tried to sleep that night.

The next morning I headed to the office with a heavy heart and feeling like a total failure. I loved Pete a lot, and didn't care to see anyone in so much trouble that they had to be fired. But I also knew that after a lot of prayer, following Scriptural principles, and doing everything I knew to do, Pete had to go. I left word with Pete's secretary that when Pete came into the office I wanted to see him.

About 11:15 that morning, I got a call. It was Pete sounding really dejected. "Tom, I've just got to talk to you." "Well, Pete, I want to talk with you, too. Where are you?" Pete hesitated, as though he was trying to figure out where he was, and finally said, "I'm at a pay phone at the corner of Fox and 4th." I knew the location a few blocks from the office. "Pete, that's out in the open and it's pouring rain." "Yeh, I know. Can I come see you?" My heart ached. "Of course. Get over here!"

Pete was a soaking mess (and not from alcohol). "Irene, get some towels and hot coffee." After we dried him off and got something hot inside him, I urged him to sit down. "No Tom, I'll get your chair dirty and wet, and I've caused you enough trouble"—and then Pete broke down and wept with sobs that were more agonizing than I think I had ever heard.

Finally, I gently pushed Pete into a chair. Then, as Pete buried his head in his hands and wept, he blurted out, "Yesterday they sentenced my oldest son—he's 22, you never met him—to life in prison without parole, ever, for murder. It was in another state so you never knew." "Pete, why didn't you ever tell me? How can I help?" was all that I could say.

"You've been kind. And you've cared. But Tom, I'm so ashamed. I've failed as a dad, I've failed as a husband, and I've failed you and my people. I'm so, oh so, ashamed." "Pete, when did all of this start?"

> I knew the answer even before Pete blurted it out, "About 18 months ago, my son was arrested. That phone call from the police in the middle of the night will haunt me for the rest of my life. I just couldn't handle it. And I couldn't tell anyone—it was so terrible."
>
> We never got to discuss my reason for calling Pete into my office. I didn't fire Pete. Instead we talked about Jesus Christ and how the Lord sometimes doesn't make tragedy or changes go away, instead He provides the strength and support to live through those changes and in some cases, learn and grow from the experiences. To put it simply, God can move the dysfunctional wall.
>
> Well, Pete got his act together at work. It was obvious that he had a heavy heart, but he performed well. Then he resigned to take another job and move his three kids to a place in that other state where they could visit his oldest son in prison.
>
> But the story doesn't end there. Six years later, after I had moved on to another company, another state, and another role in life, my office phone rang. At the other end of the call was a strong cheerful voice. It was Pete. "Tom, I just had to track you down to tell you that God has really changed my life. Yes, the kids miss their mom, but they're doing great and my oldest son will always be in prison, but we see him several times a month and I'm now a vice-president in a good company and the work is tough (we're downsizing). But most of all, I walk with the Lord, and He really is my strength. I just called to say thanks for following the Scripture and never giving up on me and for introducing me to Jesus Christ."

Here's a case when someone had run into—no, crashed into—the dysfunctional wall. Too much tragedy, too many blind-sided changes, and Pete had run out of cope.

Note: Pete was confronted with a reality check that moved him in a different direction than up the steps to the dysfunctional wall. In fact, he actually came back down the steps to "this change is unacceptable" and took the other fork. Figure 8.3 demonstrates the alternative.

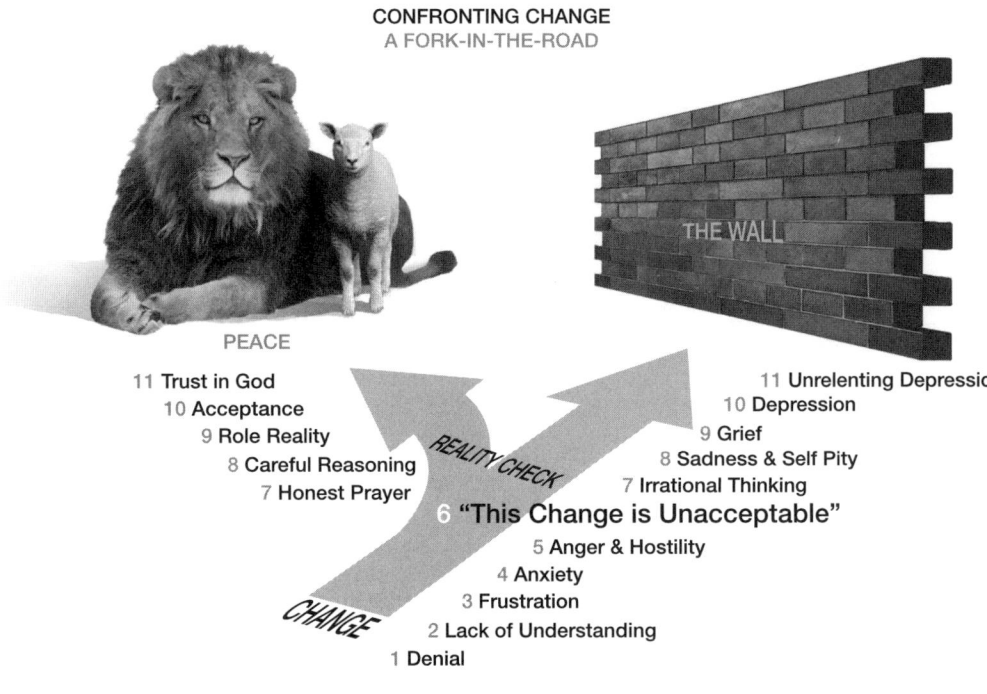

FIGURE 8.3

The fork toward Peace departs no later than "This Change is Unacceptable" on the steps toward the dysfunctional wall. In a mind and heart scenario it is when a person comes to his senses. But the real steps toward Peace are intertwined with the soul. Table 8.4 expands on turning Cope into Hope as you follow a genuine faith in the Lord that provides the courage to confront any change.

	ACTIONS	EXPLANATION
7	Honest Prayer	Honest and fervent prayer should be a way of life for the Christ-follower, but we don't always live that way. Instead, God is brought in to help face inevitable change when we experience frustration, anxiety, and anger. Nonetheless, He listens, helps, and calms in a way that only the Christ-follower comprehends.
8	Careful Reasoning	When God is involved, He directs so that your heart and mind don't control you. He helps temper your emotions so spirit-led thinking and careful reasoning provide support in facing change.
9	Role Reality	With steps 7 and 8 in place, you can determine whether or not there is anything you can do about the change. And if not, turn it over to the Lord and move on. If you find that you do have a role to play in the change, God will lead you to take the right actions in addressing the change.
10	Acceptance	By the time you have moved through steps 7, 8, and 9, even if the change has blind-sided you, even if it is traumatic, even if it is filled with risk, even if it is severely disliked, you can accept that the change is real and seek to learn from it and use it for eternal results.
11	Trust in God	At this stage, you recognize that God is sovereign, that His ways are beyond understanding, and that He is in control of all things. This fork-in-the-road doesn't necessarily bring good results from either the mind or the heart, but trusting in Christ brings a peace that is beyond your understanding.

TABLE 8.4

Notice that an individual usually goes through the first five steps/signs toward hitting the wall before choosing a branch in the road. Why would you, when confronted with an unlikable change, have to experience denial, lack of understanding, frustration, anxiety, anger, and hostility? For most people—even the mature Christ-Follower—the first reaction is based on self. And self is allied with getting the facts and feeding our emotions. Then when reason and feeling give way to the realization that I can't handle it, faith takes over.

Think about it. How much less anguish would a person encounter, no matter how severe the change, if he were dominated by Christ-centeredness? Why not start with step 7 (Honest Prayer)? Then, no matter what the change—planned and predictable, subtle and sporadic, accelerated and heavy, or blind-sided and traumatic—peace about it would come quickly.

Section 2 Chapter 8 PonderPoints

The Bible says,
I will praise in the name of God with song and magnify Him with thanksgiving. Psalm 69:30

Sounds pretty positive, doesn't it! But if you read the whole psalm, you'll discover where David started–hitting the dysfunctional wall. The psalm begins with this cry:
Save me, O God, for the waters have threatened my life. I have sunk in deep mire, and there is no foothold; I have come into deep waters, and a flood overflows me. I am weary with my crying; my throat is parched. Psalm 69:1-3a

1. Reflect on your life. Can you recall a time when changes were traumatic? When you were blind-sided by those changes? When your response to hitting the wall was bitterness and despair? David did a reality check and took the Fork-in-the-Road that switched his attitude toward Peace.

2. List the difficult changes you've encountered over the past year. Are you still bitter about some of them? One at a time, think about each one and prayerfully read through the following song. Does it help you take the left fork in the road?

3. Identify two out of the four principles presented in chapter 7 that you should work on to help you increase your resiliency and help you avoid hitting the wall.

NO.	SUMMARIZE THE PRINCIPLE IN YOUR OWN WORDS

4. Go back to the RealityCase about Pete. Then complete the following table.

CHANGE THAT PETE ENCOUNTERED	ATTEMPTED REMEDY	SUCCESSFUL?
Slipped Performance No. 1		
Slipped Performance No. 2		
Violent Wife & Messy Divorce		
Slipped Performance No. 3		
Son Convicted and Imprisoned		

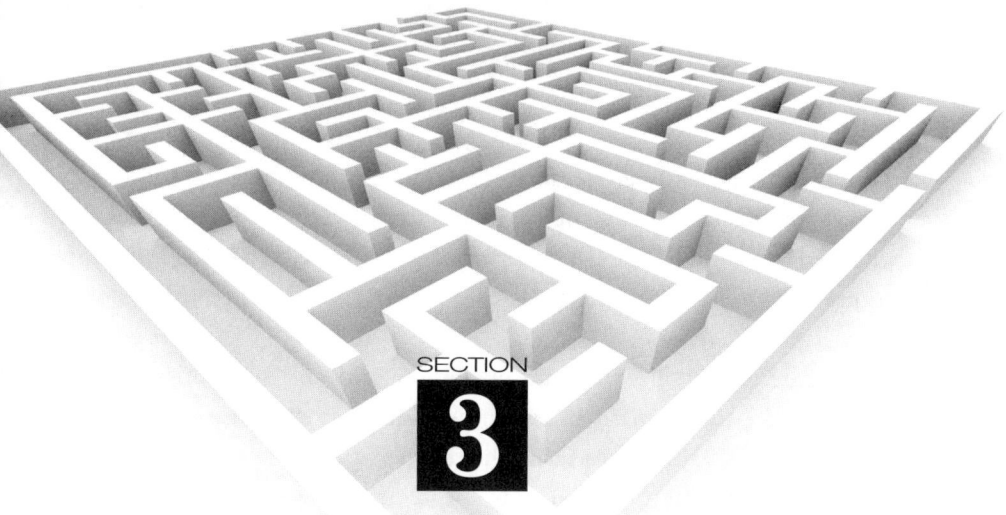

SECTION

3

USING THE SPIRITUAL DIMENSION
to navigate better

Did you realize that God was the author of change? Daniel 2:21 says, "He changes times and seasons; he sets up kings and deposes them." Think about it! The universe contracts and expands; the leaves change color; all forms of life are born, grow, decay, and pass; you increase in knowledge over the years, and change is happening no matter where you look.

Sections I & II have focused primarily on the mind (factual) and heart (emotional) dimensions of change mazes and labyrinths. The insights examined there are designed to help you manage yourself when confronted with change by determining the kind of change it is, sorting facts from emotions, recognizing the shapers involved, and knowing yourself well enough to deal with the maze.

But let's face it. My experiences with clients, students, family, brothers and sisters in Christ, and life itself have taught me that a two-dimensional solution is not enough. Navigating change mazes, especially when they have become so complex that they become labyrinths that close in, require more. You may have: will, time, intuition, personality, change capacity, energy, confidence, experience, knowledge, and perseverance. Yet with all of that innate capability, and even if you do have the nav tips written on your sleeve, you can still be overwhelmed by some changes. (When I was a quarterback, I had the plays written on my wrist-band. When the coach used a code to send in a play, I could look it up. It was like a map.)

This section applies the third dimension; faith in Jesus Christ. It should help you navigate the maze somewhat like using a satellite in the sky overhead that can see you, what's ahead, and the corridors that surround you.

The soul (faith) dimension adds a whole new view for navigating change mazes. This added set of insights and nav tips focuses on the Lord's role in showing you the map of the maze, equipping you with His perspective, and helping you move beyond the facts and emotions to the eternal view.

At some point, dealing with change raises more challenging questions. Most of what we have discussed so far is how to navigate when you are confronted with change. But as a Christ-follower, you may be asking more questions. Why can't God just let things be the way they are? Why does He give me the options to change or not change? Why does He allow so many changes all at once? How can I tap into God's understanding of the tough mazes I'm facing? Where is He leading me? When can I rest? Will He keep me in this labyrinth forever? How does all of this effort of finding my way through change after change reflect His Glory back to Him?

Not all of those questions will be answered here. It is more important that you develop an ever-increasing and satisfying perspective of God's use of changes in your life. As you focus more on the spiritual dimension of changes you encounter, you'll begin to recognize the fruitful outcomes that God has planned for you.

CHAPTER NINE
The Ultimate Change:
Becoming a Christ-Follower

When I was a teenager, I watched a change that has impacted my life ever since. Here's the story.

The New Bill Rettgen

Bill Rettgen was a family man. He was faithful to his wife, loved his kids, and made a good living that provided a modest home and nourishing food for the family.

His business made a lot of demands on his time. In a town of 650 people, he was the only "oil man" to provide heating oil and diesel fuel to the town's residents and the farms within a 25-mile radius. Even though he delivered on a scheduled basis, he was always being called out in the middle of the night (so it seemed) to fill someone's tank. The farming community had needs around the clock. It wasn't uncommon that Bill would get a call for help between midnight and 4:00 A.M., so he'd have to get up, get dressed, drive 20 miles, stand in the cold while the fuel was being pumped into someone's tank, and drive home. And that standing around being cold was the root of the problem (in Bill's mind). As he'd stand there in the dark, shivering from the cold, usually alone because the farmer stayed in his warm house, Bill would slip a bottle out from under the truck seat and warm himself with warming liquor.

He was always able to handle the drive back home, but then the liquor would take effect. There were times that he couldn't even find his way to the kitchen door from the garage. Several times Alice, his wife, would find him "asleep" in the snow where he had fallen. But Bill could hold his liquor. By morning he'd be able to get up, clean up, eat a big breakfast with lots of black coffee, and greet his girls as they started their day. And he did a good job—on the job. People were really pleased with his fine service and above all, the low prices on his oil.

Alice and the girls were devout Christians. They attended a little church in town (where I also attended) that met both the spiritual and social needs of Susan (14), Dorothy (11), and Jane (4), and Mom. But Bill didn't seem to show any interest in church stuff. He had gone to church—or had been forced to go to church—as a kid, but once he got established on his own, he said he really didn't need it. He knew many of our church members, and lots of them (who were his customers) just wouldn't pay their bills on time. Some of them were as much as eight months behind with their payments, so he had to borrow money at hefty interest rates to keep his oil and diesel fuel on hand. In fact, he was pretty bitter about church and church people.

Alice was wise. She'd always suggest to Bill that he join them when they went to church and was gracious when he'd storm out of the house muttering that it wasn't for him—or any real self-made man. But she never pushed. She honored him as her husband and above all, she prayed (along with the girls and other Christ-followers).

One evening during supper, Alice mentioned that the church had a special speaker coming. He, Missionary Ford, was going to talk about Christ's love and how unconditional it was. Bill skipped dessert and moved towards the door. As always, he said he didn't care what

Alice and the girls did about such sissy stuff, but they should leave him out of it. When she mentioned that is was for people who didn't go to church (and wouldn't be interested in going to a regular Sunday worship service), Bill stomped out of the house to make an emergency delivery at Harvey Siles place—way out at the very edge of his territory.

The church was pretty full—mostly with Christians from the churches around the county. Lots of music. Some of it wasn't too good, but people seemed to enjoy it. Then there were the "testimonies." People who had experienced the Lord's work in their lives told about it. And then Missionary Ford talked. He didn't really preach, he just read from the Scriptures and told how God loved us so much that He didn't want us to live in Hell forever after we die. Ford really spoke softly when he explained about God's gift of giving His Son, Jesus, to pay for our sins.

Just when the Missionary started to talk about how we are all sinners, there was a commotion at the door. In charged Bill. Alice and the girls were embarrassed and more than a little ashamed.

As he walked down the aisle to where they were sitting, Missionary Ford stopped talking and walked right to Bill. He shook his hand and talked to him quietly and gently—and asked Bill to join us. And Bill did it. He sat down and all of a sudden acted like he wanted to hear what Ford had to say.

Then it started all over again. Just after Missionary Ford explained about the price Christ paid for all of us and how we'd have to admit our sins and ask God's forgiveness—Bill jumped up. We all thought he was going to cause trouble. But then he calmly walked to the front of the church, got on his knees facing the first pew, and quietly began to cry.

Well, you wouldn't believe what happened to the Rettgen family after Bill sold out to Jesus Christ! The very next morning, he went to the bank and took out a loan on his fuel truck and his house. Then he went to each of his customers and paid them–in cash–what amounted to about ten percent of the money they had paid him over the past 12 months. No one understood why, so he told them and asked their

> forgiveness for stealing from them. It seems that each time he delivered oil or diesel fuel, he had added a few extra gallons to the bill that he hadn't delivered. No one ever knew! But Bill did, and above all, God did! And then Bill told them what had happened to him in church that night. He was now a new man. And Jesus was the reason. Bill knew he'd been forgiven and would live forever–in Heaven, not Hell! He then begged them to give their lives to Christ. Most people thought he was still drinking (which he never did again), but a few people did just what Bill asked them to do. In fact, their names are written in God's book of life, probably right beside Bill's.

Bill Rettgen was a man who was lost for eternity; not because he drank alcohol or because he didn't go to church. It was because Bill did not have a personal relationship with Jesus Christ. But God found Bill and Bill found Christ. Wow! What a change! And I was privileged to witness it.

The approach to day-to-day change issues for the Christ-follower should reflect the spiritual transformation in his life. Christ coming into Bill's life instantly changed both his heart and mind. And those changes brought about changed behavior and actions. They also gave Bill a totally new perspective of the change mazes and the labyrinth changes that God put in his path. Knowing that God either created or allowed changes in his life, Bill was confident that the same Lord would either guide him through the maze or give him peace about getting stuck in it.

There will be times when facts (mind) and emotional (heart) changes swamp, impact, overrun, surprise, anger, scare, trouble, tempt, challenge, delight, excite, harm, injure, and/or insult the Christ-follower. During these times, the living Christ sooths, calms, and brings hope within His follower to turn all changes to His Glory. The dominance of the Lord literally overshadows the facts and the emotions.

Frankly, this is the most important chapter in this book! The RealityCase described the ultimate change of an individual receiving Christ as his personal

Savior. In an instant, when you confess that you are a sinner, acknowledge that Jesus is God's Son and that He paid for your sins on the cross, believe that Jesus is the only way to eternal life, and turn yourself completely over to Him—you become a child of God and will live with Him through all eternity. That change is an all-encompassing transition from lost to found, damned to saved, rejected to accepted, Hell-bound to Heaven-bound, stressed to calmed, conflicted to peaceful, fearful to joyful, and dead to alive. The change to being Christ-centered gives the Christ-follower an eternal perspective instead of a *this world* view of the other changes in your life. Figure 9.1 demonstrates just a few of those other changes.

AS-IS		TO-BE
Dead		Alive
Lost	TRANSITION	Found
Damned		Saved
Rejected		Accepted
Guilty		Forgiven
Hell-Bound		Heaven-Bound
Stressed		Calmed
Conflicted		Peaceful
Fearful		Bold
Sad		Joyful
Self-Centered		Christ-Centered
Loved		Loved
Causing God Sadness		Causing God Joy
Focused on Mind & Heart Views		Focused on Soul Views

FIGURE 9.1

If you forget everything else written in this book, but remember and believe these quotes from the Scriptures, you'll be well on the way to knowing Christ as your anchor in the storm of change.

> For God so loved the world that He gave His only begotten Son, that whoever believes in Him shall not perish, but have eternal life.
>
> John 3:16
>
> I have been crucified with Christ; and it is no longer I who live, but Christ lives in me; and the life which I now live in the flesh I live by faith in the Son of God, who loved me and gave Himself up for me.
>
> Galatians 2:20
>
> Therefore, if anyone is in Christ, he is a new creature; the old things passed away; behold, new things have come.
>
> II Corinthians 5:17

Section 3 Chapter 9 PonderPoints

1. Recall a change labyrinth that you navigated successfully. You made the right decisions and you chose the right corridors along the way with only a few wrong turns. Briefly describe the situation, your challenge, and the outcome.

Now use the following table to describe the three dimensions involved.

DIMENSION DESCRIPTIONS

FACTS	EMOTIONS	FAITH

2. In the Scriptures, Paul records that he was stuck in a labyrinth. He says, ". . . there was given me a thorn in the flesh. . . I implored the Lord three times that it might leave me. And He has said to me, 'My grace is sufficient for you, for power is perfected in weakness.'"

II Corinthians 12:7–9

Have you entered a change maze that you can't get out of? Have you realized that God's grace is sufficient to give you peace while you're in it? Describe the situation and then complete the following table.

DIMENSION DESCRIPTIONS

FACTS	EMOTIONS	FAITH

Check the box that needs more work on your part.

3. Think about the transition points shown in Figure 9.1. Add others that happened as a result of your choosing to be a Christ-follower. Then check Yes for all of those changes you have sensed in your life.

BEFORE CHRIST I WAS...	AFTER CHRIST I AM...	YES!
Dead	Alive	
Lost	Found	
Damned	Saved	
Rejected	Accepted	
Guilty	Forgiven	
Hell-Bound	Heaven-Bound	
Stressed	Calmed	
In Conflict	At Peace	
Fearful	Bold	
Sad	Joyful	
Self-centered	Christ-centered	
Loved	Loved	
Causing God Sadness	Bringing God Joy	
Focused on Mind & Heart Views	Focused on Soul Views	

CHAPTER TEN
The Resulting Change:
From Self-Centered to Christ-Centered

The change to becoming a Christ-follower doesn't always bring with it the instant switch in thoughts and actions like it did for Bill Rettgen. God uses many ways to transition you to becoming what He wants you to be. I spent several years working for ITT. We often joked that ITT stood for It Takes Time. Our Lord often works that way, too. Here are a few questions to get you thinking about where you were, where you are, and where He wants you to go: Do you ever experience a tug of war between your self-interests and what you know God wants you to do? What do you think of the statement, "I've earned it and I can do whatever I want with it?" How do you respond when you are blindsided by a change that messes with your plans?

Since the fall of Adam, humankind has placed self at its center. Watch a child from birth through preschool. The crying, the demanding, the begging, the foot stomping, the tugging on tired parents (and grandparents) are accompanied by chants of "mine," "gim'me," and "I want . . ." As kids grow older, the techniques are refined to the art of manipulation and couched in smiles, drippy sweet words, hugs-for-candy, mock cooperation, and requests to "look at me." As teens mature into adults, their methods become both subtle and direct.

A look back at the 1960s shows the emergence of the "Me Generation," known for their blatant self-centeredness expressed straightforwardly in the motto, "If it feels good, do it." The growing cultural acceptance of self-indulgence has marched on unabated since then. But remember, this is not a recent phenomenon, this love of self. At the beginning of earth-time, an account in the Bible describes the jealousy between the first two brothers that ever lived. One was so devastated by the fact that God didn't approve of his offering that he killed his brother who had given an acceptable offering (the first murder on earth, recorded in Genesis 4).

The Apostle Paul in the New Testament, who had a dramatic ultimate change when the Lord took over his life, still had a continual battle with self-centeredness. He wrote that he had to die to self every day. Each day of his life, Paul had to ask God to dominate his mind and heart. He was so enriched by his love for Jesus that he continually pursued the changed life of a Christ-centered man.

Down through history this self-centeredness thrived. For instance, one of the long-lasting assumptions of Aristotle was that the sun revolved around the earth. In 390 BC, Aristotle proclaimed that the earth was the center of the universe. You may dismiss this kind of thinking because people back then didn't know any better. "After all, they also believed the world was flat. As grand and intellectual as Aristotle was, he just didn't know any better." Well, over the centuries, philosophies and religions—particularly the Christian church—expanded on this thinking. If the earth is the center of God's creation, and humans are made in the image of God, then the universe must revolve around humans. Note: The Church operated on this assumption until the century when the Reformation started a God-centered change.

The transition to thinking the sun was the center of the solar system instead of the earth was tough. Take Galileo, for instance.

> Galileo (1564-1642) was famous. His work had already disproved Aristotle's (384-322 BC) incorrect fact that heavy objects fell faster than light objects. Galileo's findings led to his appointment as philosopher and mathematician to the grand duke of Tuscany. During a visit to Rome (1611), he spoke persuasively that, "the earth is not the center of the solar system but the sun was instead. And the earth actually revolves around the sun and rotated on its own axis."
>
> This thesis put him at odds with Aristotelian professors and led to Galileo's line of thinking being declared false and erroneous by the

Church in 1616. Obtaining permission to write about this new idea so long as he discussed it noncommittally, he wrote his Dialogue Concerning the Two Chief World Systems (1632).Though considered a masterpiece, it enraged the Jesuits, and Galileo was tried before the Inquisition, found guilty of heresy, and forced to recant. He spent the rest of his life under house arrest, continuing to write and conduct research even after going blind in 1637.[6]

What is fascinating is that a scientific fact rattled the theologians of the day. A closer look links the idea that "the earth is the center of the universe" to "man is the center of the universe." This erroneous bridge continues to be the basis of humanist philosophy. Unfortunately this concept has made its way into Christian circles and too frequently the marvelous truth, "Christ died for me," stops there—instead of exclaiming the whole truth, "Christ died for me to glorify Himself!"

Now, what does this have to do with change? When the ultimate change described in Chapter 9 takes place in you—when the Christ-centeredness takes over—a totally new person emerges. It's like the ugly, earth-hugging, wiggly, food-devouring, slow, worm (caterpillar) that goes through a change to become a beautiful, free, non-earthbound, quick, productive, flower-flitting butterfly.

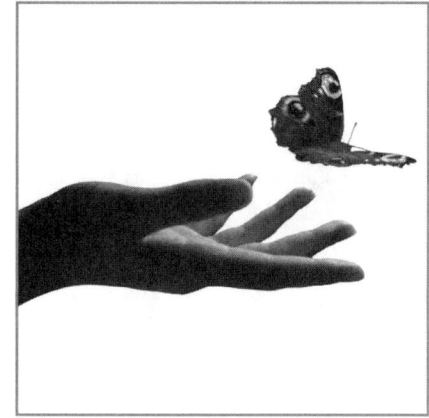

6 *Encyclopedia Britannica 2003 Ready Reference*

Think about it! If you are controlled by your emotions, you'll usually respond to the change based on what it means to you. Businesses encourage their people to initiate changes based on WIFM (What's In It For Me) to motivate employees, customers, suppliers, and others. And if you are intent on initiating a change, it is because it benefits you and your world—unless you are Christ-centered. Simply stated, if you are directed by your heart and mind only, you're usually self-centered. (Most people will deny that fact.) The following RealityCase illustrates the difference between being controlled by the mind/heart and being controlled by the soul.

RealityCase

A Tale of Two Preachers

The area was booming! What was once a quiet, sleepy, comfortable, slow-moving, church-going, family-centered, moderately priced community was becoming a big buck, fast-paced, fine living attraction for the well-to-do. The large lake, the wandering streams, and the rolling tree-covered hills provided a comfortable setting for retiring executives and spouses who wanted to get out of the hubbub of the corporate rat race.

Lake Norman was also close enough to several large metropolises for high-energy people to commute. Yet the distances were far enough to really separate the fast-paced work from slowed-down living. It was an ideal setting for Cheke and me, since much of my work could be done via the Internet and teleconferencing. And when I was required to meet with clients who literally lived around the globe, I'd have to travel no matter where I lived. Besides, if the client wanted to meet in a retreat setting, what better place was there than our home?

Some people had two places, one on the lake or golf course and one where they worked. This oasis provided an ideal place to escape on weekends and extended vacations.

This upscale intrusion into such a comfortable and history-filled community meant change. And not all of it was good. For one thing, this traditional, church-centered area now had more folk who weren't churched than those who were. The growth brought three socioeconomic groups into the community: the well-to-dos who were buying up the land and building their homes, the skilled tradesmen who met the demands for construction, and the laborers who provided the strength and brawn to make it all happen.

Miles away, in the New York area, Rev. Carl Loche began to think that his ministry at Second Community Church (SCC) had gone about as far as he could take it. The church was running well. The up and outers who had been the target of his eight years of ministry were nicely in line. The committees were running well, the church debt had been paid off, and there was a real sense of satisfaction in the church. Besides meeting their budget, they were sending five percent of their offerings to the foreign mission field and they were providing the financial support for a start-up church in Harlem. Although he had never been there, he was pleased with the reports that Pastor Amos was now preaching to 40+ each Sunday. And Carl had heard that the Friday soup kitchen was a real success! Yes, God had really blessed his ministry.

Then Carl heard from one of his deacons, Terry, about Lake Norman. Besides having great golf courses and a marvelous lake, they really needed more churches! Since Terry had built his future retirement home on the lake, he suggested that Carl and his wife might enjoy a week of vacation there. Carl and Nancy jumped at it.

Carl had the reputation of being a successful leader and church developer. Lake Norman might be a place for him to start a new ministry and set himself up for a truly delightful retirement location (after all, he was nearing 60). So during that week of vacation, he and Nancy went to work. They met with key developers around Lake Norman. And Carl played golf—both to check out the golf courses and to check out the golfers. He found that many of his newly found companions were just like the people at SCC, well-off and needing the church as a social center and stabilizing force in the community.

By the end of the week, Carl had contacted the church back home and arranged for one of his associate pastors to cover the Sunday morning service for him. He had organized a meeting at one of his newly found friend's homes to talk about organizing a new church—which he would lead.

Carl knew that he had to do it right. These were sharp business people who could analyze the opportunities quickly. They would also evaluate him as their potential pastor. So he opened the meeting with prayer, shared from the Scriptures about the commission to "go out and reach others," and then launched into his background. He had pastored several large churches along the East Coast. Each of them had grown under his ministry. He even named several well-known athletes, business leaders, entertainers, and politicians which he had baptized. John chronicled his ministerial journey and outlined his many successes.

Some of us were impressed and John could sense it. As the meeting progressed, he became bolder. If they wanted him to start right away, he could actually turn the SCC pulpit over to those under him and he could fly in each weekend to start cottage church services. But he'd need a place to stay and funds would be required for travel.

As the discussion continued, he brought up the desire to buy property on the lake and become a member at one of the premier golf courses. But being a minister, he just didn't have those kinds of resources. Maybe this new church could arrange a deal for land he could buy and talk one of the developers into giving him a golf course membership. And maybe a developer would be willing to give some land in the center of this community for a new church.

During the next week, after Carl and Nancy had returned to New York to await the response to his plan, several of us began to challenge one another. In fact, some of the discussions were quite heated. The main debate was whether this was the way to start a church. No one doubted the need. But to some, the approach seemed troublesome. As we recounted the meeting, some thought Carl had emphasized his own interests ahead of the desire for a church. Others thought he was just being wise in making sure his needs were being met. Over several weeks, the group began to disband. I was asked to notify Rev. Locke that the timing just wasn't right and that although we needed a new church, his approach didn't fit our ideas of how a church should be started. Carl and Nancy were not only disappointed, they were terribly upset with the turn of events. Their hopes and plans had fallen apart.

Several months later a quiet-spirited man and his wife showed up at Lake Norman. They went from door to door asking people about their relationship with Jesus Christ and whether or not they had a church home. If they weren't involved in a church, or wanted to know more about the Lord, Pastor Darren (Waite) invited them to join a group of people with similar interests. They were planning to meet on Sunday evenings at an empty store building near the lake.

That first Sunday evening was really interesting. About 30 people showed up; some were people who really loved Jesus Christ and others were just curious. Darren started the evening by introducing some young people from a nearby community who did a reasonable job of leading with upbeat music about God's Love. Then Pastor Darren and his wife explained that they had started churches in several similar communities—and they were asking God if He wanted them to do it at Lake Norman.

After more music, Darren told us about the role of the church in God's plan. It was to be the bride of Christ and had two primary objectives: first, to lead people to know Christ and receive Him as their Lord and Savior for all eternity; second, to teach and grow believers to glorify God and do His work in every part of their lives. Pastor Darren emphasized that he didn't know for sure what God wanted done at Lake Norman, so he asked everyone to pray hard that God would make His plan known, understood, and followed. Then the meeting was over. We stood around visiting and getting acquainted—and agreed that meeting the following Sunday night would be a good idea. Darren said he'd be around to help. Some of us asked if he'd lead again and he agreed. But then he said something interesting. He wanted everyone to invite others to the meeting—and to make sure that they didn't just limit their invitation list to people like themselves. Christ came to prove God's love for everyone from every station in life, and the church should make sure that it touched all kinds of people from every socioeconomic group.

Fast forwarding about three years finds that Lake Norman Community Church (LNCC) has recently upgraded to a fourth storefront to accommodate more people each week. The new church's phone is ringing off the wall in response to ads on local TV and radio. People are seeking and finding Christ as Savior, people as true friends, and a spiritual basis for their lives. Pastor Darren isn't too polished as a preacher, but his love for the Lord and his love for the people has radiated throughout the community. He laughs about his lousy golf game, but he enjoys being invited to join other men in chasing that white ball into the woods or losing it in the lake.

As for LNCC, they recently bought 30 acres of land for a new church facility. It isn't on the lake—that would cost too much—but it is centrally located and easily accessible for the entire spectrum of people in the area. In fact, the first thing they decided to do was build a soccer field for the laborers and kids in the community to show that the church, along with their Lord, really cares about their future and their families.

Pastor Darren has indicated that in another year or two he'll be moving on . . . going wherever God wants him to go to show the love of Christ by starting more churches. And he will continue to preach that "the church is the Body of Believers, not the facility they worship in!"

Both Carl and Darren were involved in change. From what the RealityCase presented, who was more self-centered and who was more Christ-centered? One of the objectives of this book is to help readers find satisfaction instead of disappointment in change. Pastor Darren was soul driven. His contentment came from having an eternal view of what he was doing. Carl wasn't so blessed.

Instead of seeing that God was at work in his life, he took the Lord out of his equation for success—and that resulted in his being disappointed and angry.

God's Word records numerous incidents that show the difference between self-centered and God-centered lives. Remember Joseph? The spoiled little kid in a family of ten older brothers? They kidnapped him, sold him to slave traders, and told their father that a wild animal had killed him. Joseph lived through it all and became so successful that those same brothers came begging for food when there was a famine in their homeland. When they discovered that the man who was providing food for them and their families was the brother they had abused, they had every right to be afraid for their lives.

But Joseph had a totally different view:

> Now do not be grieved or angry with yourselves, because you sold me here, for God sent me before you to preserve life. **Genesis 45:5**

And later when his brothers showed their fear and begged his forgiveness, he consoled them:

> Do not be afraid for am I in God's place? As for you, you meant evil against me, but God meant it for good in order to bring abut this present result, to preserve many people alive. **Genesis 50:19-20**

Instead of revenge, there was help. Instead of hatred, there was love. Instead of anger, there was forgiveness. Joseph could have resented the changes his brothers had imposed on his life years before. Both the facts and the emotions justified that position. But his soul provided him with the insight that God had a larger plan—an eternal plan—and Joseph not only accepted but thrived in his changed circumstances.

There are so many changes in today's world—some of them acceptable and some of them totally unacceptable. The speed, distaste, and magnitude of change can overwhelm you. How do you sort and cope with this avalanche of change? This chapter closes with an example of how frustrated I can be when I know I'm caught in a collection of change mazes and have no hope of finding the exit. Even though this episode happened more than 10 years ago, I'm repeatedly reminded of the question that really provides the answer to many of my frustrations.

I arrived home from the office—late for supper as usual. Anger, frustration, and fatigue were written all over my face and reflected in my body language. Sensing the situation, Cheke asked me to tell her about what was bothering me.

I unloaded: "Senseless clients at work, traffic jams on the way home, news on the radio that the country is going to war in a foreign land, our life savings eroding as the market drops, politics are controlled by vultures, the morality of the country is literally going to hell, and more cutbacks are rumored at several of my clients! Nothing stays right. Why are there so many changes going on?"

Tim, my young adult son looked at me with disgust and compassion. "Dad, why are you so upset? Lighten up! Does your worrying about any of these issues have eternal value?"

Here are two nav tips right from Jesus Himself.

NAVIGATION TIP:

Do not be worried about your life . . . Look at the birds of the air, that they do not sow, nor reap, nor gather into barns and yet your heavenly Father feeds them. Are you not worth much more than they?

Matthew 6:25-26

NAVIGATION TIP:

Do not let your heart be troubled; believe in God, believe also in Me.

John 14:1

Section 3 Chapter 10 PonderPoints

1. No one else can honestly determine if you are primarily Christ-centered or self-centered. And sometimes you may not even know for sure. These PonderPoints are for you to answer personally and privately. You may not even want to mark the page (so no one else can see). But make a mental note as you ask yourself who motivates you in each of the following cases.

   a. Your position at work or your performance at school (Christ or you)

   b. Your reputation at work or at school (Christ or you)

   c. Your choice of a spouse (Christ or you)

   d. The kind of car you drive or hope to drive (Christ or you)

   e. The home you live in or hope to live in (Christ or you)

   f. The amount of money you give to your church (Christ or you)

   g. The good deeds you do (Christ or you)

h. The people you invite to your home for dinner (Christ of you)

i. Your leisure time (Christ or you)

j. The amount of time you spend reading God's Word (Christ or you)

k. The time you spend in prayer (Christ or you)

l. The roles you take on at church (Christ or you)

m. Your longing to go to Heaven (Christ or you)

n. Your attitude about life (Christ or you)

o. What your neighbors think of you (Christ or you)

p. The time you spend helping the poor (Christ or you)

q. Your giving to charity (Christ or you)

And the list goes on. What does this have to do with navigating change mazes? Your responses can help you determine whether you think of God as your copilot or as your pilot. The person in the right seat of an airplane (copilot) is guided, coached, directed, and commanded by the person in the left seat. I suggest that you'll do a lot better navigating change mazes, especially those that have become labyrinths, if you seek Christ first. The Scripture says, "But seek first His kingdom and His righteousness, and all these things will be add to you." Matthew 6:33.

CHAPTER ELEVEN
Now You're Equipped to Decide:
Change or Not Change

Are you a good decision-maker? Or do you do everything you can to avoid it? Can you remember times when you faced a change maze where you had the option to change or not change? Even more challenging, have there been situations where you were asked to be part of a change that you considered unacceptable? Did the complexity of the change maze in front of you pose so many unknowns and risks that you didn't want to enter?

In this book we've dealt with the characteristics of the several kinds of change mazes. Hopefully you understand the issues surrounding blind-side changes that turn mazes into labyrinths. And you know the steps that could lead you to hitting the dysfunctional wall. Most importantly, you know the power of the ultimate change by giving yourself to Christ and making the change from self-centered for Christ-centered. With that preparation, you should now be equipped to stand up to decisions about whether to Change or Not Change.

During my years of focusing on change, I've been asked many times, "How do I know if I should go along with, be part of, or resist change?" "What if I'll lose my job or my spouse or my family or (something else of great value) if I don't become part of an unacceptable change?" "What if the change is so counter to my walk with Christ that I just can't do it?"

If you're looking for a prescriptive set of steps that will get you through such difficult challenges, don't read any further. I'm the first to admit that I don't have pat answers. What I do have, however, is Jesus Christ within me; He can take over and navigate for and through me. Hopefully a few mini-RealityCases will set the stage. Then we'll examine some tips that help me make decisions about changes when I really do have options.

 3 Mini-RealityCases

To Change or Not to Change

TO CHANGE OR QUIT

A friend of mine, Robert, was a very successful physician with a specialty in OBGYN (obstetrics and gynecology). The rumor was that he had delivered more than half the babies in the city. Although he didn't have the best bed-side manners, he was highly respected, extremely competent, and everyone knew that he cared deeply for the well being of mother and child. He also had a strong commitment to his faith in Jesus Christ and was a tireless laborer for the Lord in his work, his church, his community, and his world. He used vacations for short-term mission trips to Third World countries.

The change I'm about to describe didn't blind-side him. Robert saw it coming. Pressure was mounting for him and his colleagues to perform abortions. There had been lengthy discussions, official meetings with the other partners of the clinic, and meetings with the hospital boards where they served as physician staff. And then his opposition to abortion was overridden. The clinic and the hospitals agreed that they would perform abortions. They also agreed to a lengthy set of rules to make sure they were doing it legally and with minimal risk to the mother.

Robert was told that he would have to change from his personal no abortion policy to comply with the decision. He would have to perform abortions. His appeals and reasoning that abortion was taking a life that God created were turned down by his partners. He was given the options: comply or leave.

Within 48 hours of the rejection of his appeal, Robert resigned from the clinic and resigned from the hospital staff positions he held. He personally contacted each of his patients, past and present, and told them of his decision and the reason for it. Robert took one more step; he took early retirement and let his physician license lapse.

I interviewed Robert about his decision process. Here are the key points I gleaned from him.

Robert was an avid Christ-follower. He had sold out to Jesus Christ and was committed to honoring Him and serving Him. Therefore he had a strong set of nonnegotiable beliefs as a foundation for decisions in his life, especially moral and ethical ones.

He was well informed about the court rulings, medical facts, psychological facts, and the myths about abortion.

Robert had prayed for years about what he saw coming. He had asked others in his small group, his church, and his family to pray for wisdom when the day came that he would have to change or not change.

He and his wife had discussed at length what his options were. She was totally supportive of his position and agreed that they could live on a whole lot less than what he earned as a physician.

And finally, Robert felt real peace when he declared that he would not change. He agonized for those who were so misguided as to think abortion was some kind of solution, and he delighted in knowing that he was honoring and obeying his Lord.

TO GO OR STAY

We were finally getting comfortable. Seven years earlier when I had accepted a position with IBM in New York City, Cheke and I were overwhelmed by the changes we had to make. We were both Midwesterners, and a few visits to the Big Apple did not prepare us for the high costs, distance to work from where we thought we could afford to live, scarcity of vibrant Evangelical churches, and separation from family.

But God had been good to us. Besides actually being able to afford where we lived, I had been promoted to a location that was a whole lot nearer home. And we had settled into a good Christ-centered and God honoring church. We had two boys in school, and all three kids were healthy and happy.

For several years, I had been contacted by Mayo Clinic in Rochester, Minnesota, to find out whether I'd consider joining their team as Chief Information Officer. I had always said "no." Before going to New York, as an IBMer, I had designed several of their first research and clinical computer systems. It had been great work, but so demanding that it had almost cost me my family and emotional stability. No way did I want to get back into that rat race again.

And then they called again. After praying about it, Cheke and I decided to travel back to talk to them about the position. We came away convinced that the answer was "no"—again. The position was vaguely defined. There was a lot of internal conflict between administrative, clinical, and research computing efforts. The chairman of the board had told me that I'd be seen as an IBMer until I had the courage to order at least one computer system from a competitor. And the straw to end it all was that the offer was considerably less than I was making—and they wouldn't even pay closing costs for selling my house in New York. We decided we were not going to make the change.

But Cheke and I both felt uneasy about the decision. God kept opening doors that made us rethink the whole thing. All of a sudden, although the kids were doing just fine, I began to dwell on the fact that I was traveling so much for IBM (and loving it) that I wasn't being a good husband and dad. My job started to get boring. Our work in the church seemed to reach a plateau; it seemed that God was saying, "Well done and your work is completed here."

So we began to pray harder about it. I was leaving on a trip to the west coast and would be gone for four days. We agreed to pray about it while we were apart and said that we'd decide by Sunday evening. In the meantime we called a realtor and told her that we might be interested in selling the house. We suggested a very handsome price.

I returned on Saturday, asked people at church to pray about it, and sat down to prayerfully decide late Sunday afternoon. As we were praying, the phone rang. It was the realtor. She said, "Even though you haven't formally listed your home yet, I have a buyer who will meet your price. You know that houses aren't selling very well now. I have no idea how this came about."

That was it. We agreed to go. When we arrived at our new home in Minnesota, Cheke said out loud as the movers were carrying furniture into the kitchen, "All right God. We're here now. What do you want us to do?"

God blessed our work and our family beyond our expectations. But most of all, He expanded our ministries to further His kingdom in ways we could have never devised on our own.

TO RISK OR NOT RISK

Cheke and I have close friends, a young family with four kids ages 15, 13, 11, and 9. David and Jean homeschool, so she is swamped from dawn to midnight doing a marvelous job of being a wife, mother, teacher, and neighborhood caregiver. Dave has a demanding executive position, but he manages to squeeze out time to help with the schooling. The whole family is deeply involved with their church, and they lead a group of families who meet in their home for Bible study, fellowship, and prayer. The kids, besides excelling in their studies, are involved in sports and music lessons. And the two older boys have a lawn care and snow clearing business (that makes some extra demands on dad as well).

Our phone rang not long ago. It was Dave. "Tom and Cheke, we want you to pray for and with us. We're feeling that God may be leading us to adopt a baby—probably a minority."

My first reaction was, "David, think about the risks. Maybe the baby will have health problems. Maybe the birth parents will want the baby back after you've gotten attached to it. You two don't have enough hours in the day to get done what you're doing now. There's a big financial cost for doing this. You might neglect some of the needs your four kids have. But know that we're thrilled that you're open to the Lord's leading in your life. If He wants you to adopt a baby, He'll provide the where-with-all and way to do it. We sure will pray that

> He makes it clear to you about making such a dramatic change."
>
> They talked to other parents who had adopted babies. They visited with adoption agencies through their church. Dave and Jean asked others to pray about it with them. They attended workshops to find out what was involved before, during, and after adoption. They talked at length with their kids about it. They identified the tangible costs. And the more they prayed and the more they researched the whole thing, the more they believed that God was saying to trust Him and go for it.
>
> Today there are 5 kids in David and Jean's family. Beverly, a beautiful, fun, and sharp African-American has become the apple of her mom's, dad's, and siblings' eyes.
>
> I asked Dave recently if they thought that the adoption and Beverly were worth the risk. His answer really emphasized the spiritual dimension of change. "We didn't really consider the risk. The whole decision to make such a change in our family was a matter of faith. Once we realized that God wanted us to expand our family, we trusted Him every step of the way. And yes, it created a lot of changes. We're thrilled that we can have a part in raising Beverly and share with her the blessings of being part of a God-honoring family. But the greatest joy is knowing that our Lord is pleased and will reward our obedience to His direction."

Although there are many more examples of where people have made tough and difficult choices, these should begin to give you some insights about whether to change or not change.

Consider the following as a process or checklist you can build into your own decision-making.

CHANGE OR NOT CHANGE ✓ LIST

1. Don't let your emotions get in the way of listening to the Lord.
2. Get the facts.
3. Ask friends, experts, and other Christ-followers for their counsel.
4. Ask God to lead you as you face the maze.
5. Consider what Jesus would say about you making the change.
6. Measure the change against Scripture and your spiritual belief system.
7. Remember what you have learned from similar changes already experienced in you own life.
8. Weigh the risks.
9. Estimate what the consequences might be if you change or don't change.

FIGURE 11.1

Are you prepared to face the issues of *to change or not to change*? If you are a Christ-follower and you are willing to ask Him to help you to be Christ-centered instead of self-centered, you'll realize that you aren't making those decisions alone.

BEDROCKS

In the steps described above, there are several foundational actions that will make facing a change maze a whole lot more doable. These bedrocks provide an anchor when you are confronted with or embedded in a change maze that could cause you to risk hitting the dysfunctional wall.

ESTABLISH A WAY AND TIME TO WALK WITH GOD EACH DAY.

That means you take the time to walk with Him, talk with Him, tell Him your frustrations, and listen to His eternal wisdom. It is also a time when you can ask directions. In Lamentations 3:22-24, the Bible says, "The Lord's loving kindnesses indeed never cease. For his compassions never fail. They are new every morning; Great is Your faithfulness. 'The Lord is my portion,' says my soul, 'Therefore I have hope in Him.'"

SOAK UP THE SCRIPTURES.

God gives practical directions that provide navigation tools for every turn, wall, and blind corridor we encounter. You may think that God isn't talking with you, but He wrote a whole book about the way you should live, the way you should think, and the way you should face the unknowns of a complicated change maze. You want a navigation tool? Try this! The Bible says, "Your word is a lamp to my feet and a light to my path" Psalm 119:105.

ESTABLISH GOD-BREATHED CORE BELIEFS THAT YOU WON'T COMPROMISE.

These are the non-negotiables in your life. Lloyd, the doctor whose story was in the first mini-RealityCase, didn't really have a decision to make. His faith and his core beliefs led him to make his choice even before the Change/No Change decision had to be made. God encourages us to do that. He says in His Word, "Watch the path of your feet and all your ways will be established. Do not turn to the right nor the left." Proverbs 4:26-27a.

There is another question that often surfaces from people struggling with change: What if I make the wrong decision or choose the wrong corridor in the change maze and run into a dead-end?

Unfortunately, I have often chosen the wrong option between Change/No Change. Sometimes I charge into the change maze without following the checklist outlined earlier. The risk, uncertainty, and adventure keep me looking for the next hill to climb. But as a Christ-follower, I've never experienced a time when God has given up on me. The Bible says, "The Lord God is compassionate and gracious, slow to anger, abounding in loving kindness and truth." Exodus 34:6. He is the consummate guide because God says, "Never will I desert you; nor will I ever forsake you" Hebrews 13:5.

Sometimes God shuts the door to the maze. Even if you decide to seize an opportunity to change, He might decide to prevent you from making a mistake. It would be great if He always prevented you from taking the wrong course, but sometimes God lets you live with your mistakes in order to teach you more complete reliance on Him. The Lord wants you to learn and grow in wisdom. He uses mistake experiences as one of His teaching tools.

One of the experience lessons He used with me really got my attention. I've always like automobiles; probably too much. As I began to progress professionally, I really wanted a fine car. I changed cars too often and the cost impacted my giving to the Lord and my family a bit. But He always seemed to help us make the payments. Then I saw the chance to get an older version of the fine car I dreamed of getting. A work colleague offered to sell it to me at a price that seemed to be more than fair. I jumped on it. I didn't pray about it, I didn't discuss it with my wife (who has a sound spiritual and financial perspective), I didn't ask a wiser Christ-follower what he thought, I just did it. Since our credit was so good, I was able to get a second mortgage on our home. After I combined those funds and the money I received from selling my nearly new automobile, I agreed to pick up the fine car the next day.

That night before completing the deal, I couldn't sleep. God really got through to me. I could just hear Him say, Tom, what are you doing? Did you ask me? Did you pray about this with Cheke? Are you satisfying your ego with a car that is beyond your means? Do you think this is some kind of status symbol? Just what are your motives? How does this compare with the resources you return to Me? Is this how you manage the money I ask you to oversee?

Well, I finally convinced myself that I had given my word to someone and I couldn't go back on that, so I completed the deal. I have never had a car that cost me so much and ran so poorly. I had to pour more and more money (that we didn't have) into it to keep it running. Every time it wouldn't start in the work or church parking lots or our garage or at the shopping center, I knew I had made the wrong decision to change. I paid on that debt for two years after I got rid of the car. There is no doubt that I had decided to change when I really shouldn't have. The result didn't just impact me; it made things pretty tight for my family, too.

God has taught me more from making mistakes than from having successes. It is experiences like the fine car change maze that have helped me develop the CHANGE OR NOT CHANGE ✓LIST (Figure 11.1) that might help you.

The scriptures tell us that God is a Shepherd. And we, you and I, are His sheep. He loves us, teaches us, disciplines us, forgives us, encourages us, and even gave His Son for us so that we can be His. So when you chose to make a change that disappoints Him, remember that His plan is eternal and He doesn't ever give up on you. He may break your leg (metaphorically) as a shepherd will break the leg of a lamb to teach it to not wander, but our Lord does it to keep us close to Him.

Section 3 Chapter 11 PonderPoints

1. Identify a change decision that you are facing right now. Are there any of the nine points in the checklist that you have neglected? What are you going to do about it? Really, are you ignoring some of them because you already know what God expects of you and you don't want to hear that?

CHANGE OR NOT CHANGE ✓LIST

1. Don't let your emotions get in the way of listening to the Lord.
2. Get the facts.
3. Ask friends, experts, and other Christ-followers for their counsel.
4. Ask God to lead you as you face the maze.
5. Consider what Jesus would say about you making the change.
6. Measure the change against Scripture and your spiritual belief system.
7. Remember what you have learned from similar changes already experienced in you own life.
8. Weigh the risks.
9. Estimate what the consequences might be if you change or don't change.

2. Avoiding a change decision is to decide for the status quo. Sometimes the situation just goes away and life continues on as usual. Other times, the decision keeps coming up (like my decision to go to Mayo or stay with IBM). Think back in your life. Are there change decisions that you have been avoiding that you know you should face head on? List a few. Then go through the checklist and get them settled. Remember, you've been given a lot of tools to help you. Most of all, as a Christ-follower, you have a Guide that has the map, knows the maze inside and out, and has plans for your future.

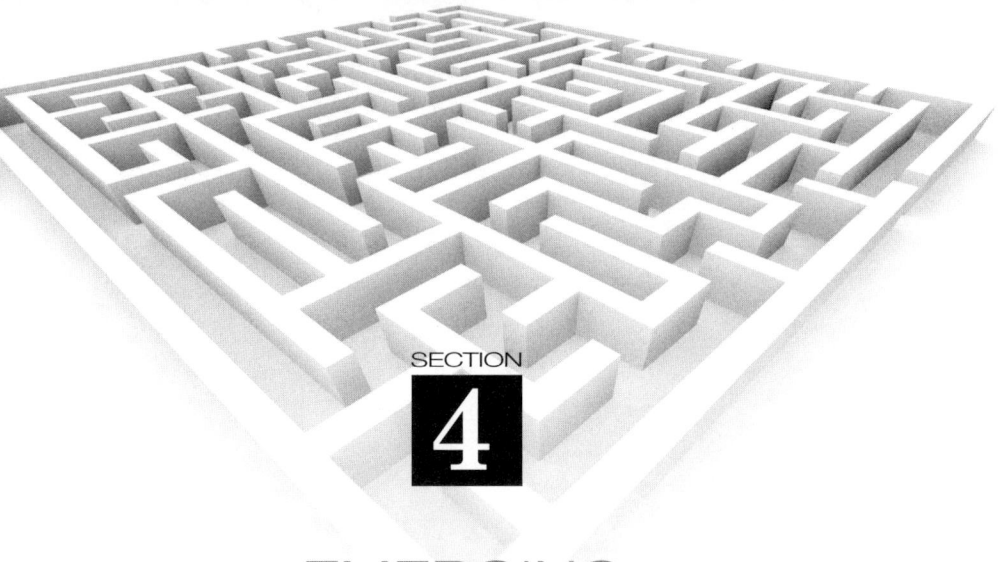

SECTION 4

EMERGING
from the maze

As a private pilot, I logged flight details after each flight. As a businessman, I found it important to do a post mortem of events and budgets after concluding a project. As a professor, I tested students to determine if they learned the material.

Now, as a consultant, I meet with clients to determine whether I am delivering results to their satisfaction. As a dad, I check with our kids from time to time to determine how the spiritual absolutes we taught them have impacted their lives. As a husband, I query my wife to find out if I can make changes that will deepen our marriage. And as a Christ-follower, I continually search God's Word to find new ways to reflect more of God's glory back to Him.

In each case the debriefings teach me about where I have been, what actions I do right, what I do wrong, and how can I change to be better prepared for mazes and labyrinths in the future. What I learn helps me understand what God is doing to help me carry out His plan for my life.

Remember early in this book we discussed that changes shape your life? This section focuses on assessing what you've learned after either emerging from a change maze or acknowledging that you're in the kind of change that doesn't end.

CHAPTER TWELVE

What Does It Mean
to Navigate Successfully?

We have examined change mazes and their characteristics. We have analyzed various kinds of change, dimensions of change as well as the impacts of change, and more. The spectrum of changers has been described as well. The intent has been to help open your mind to new ways of thinking when you encounter a change. A replay of your performance while navigating change mazes can be a meaningful tool to help you maintain hope while in the midst of change instead of just coping with change.

Remember Change Capacities (Figure 2.3)? There are people who thrive on thinking new thoughts (new idea people). Other people hang onto the status quo (resistors and slow followers). And in Chapter 15, we'll discuss those who are called to make new thoughts happen (difference makers). God has made and called people to have different perspectives as they approach change mazes. But no matter whether you are a new idea person, resistor, or difference maker, there can be real value for you in change.

Before we go further, let's understand a few concepts. First, we're talking about change, not a case of just tweaking the status quo in order to foster better sameness. Secondly, it is important that you understand what we mean by success when we refer to change. It may not be what you think. It isn't necessarily results or even the learning experience of going through the maze. Remember, this book is directed toward the individual who has experienced the ultimate change and is genuinely Christ-centered, not self-centered. To such a person, the word success is not based on personal gain but on pleasing the Lord.

We all know people who are continually interested in making changes. No matter their age, no matter their history, no matter the impact of the labyrinth or maze, they get their delight in the change by being part of the change process. These are people who get an adrenaline rush from change and may even be guilty of change for change's sake.

But there are others who are called to be difference makers. These individuals are involved because they believe in the benefits and are willing to become active in making change happen. A difference maker delights in the change because of what it can accomplish. And for the Christ-follower, spiritual results are worth the investment of energy, resources, time, and commitment.

What if you're a resistor or slow follower? You may naturally have real difficulty with change, at least the change maze(s) you're in now. How can you ever see the positive side of a change?

Before formally looking at the range of possible responses to changes that you might experience, read the following RealityCase.

Bitter or Sweet?

My mother had been on the speaking circuit across the U. S. and Canada for almost 10 years. Reva was invited to be in Who's Who among Women in America, served as national president of a women's organization that was 15,000 strong, and worked with elderly people in a local nursing home. She wrote articles for magazines, supported dad spiritually and emotionally throughout his ministry, and loved life.

And then it happened. Just before her 63rd birthday, dad died. It happened so fast. He was in intensive care for 17 days and that was it; complications from a routine surgery led to a massive heart attack, and he was gone. It was a blindside change with real momentum: fast and heavy.

After burying her beloved husband of 41 years, Reva went to their little house to remember, pray, and weep with a heavy heart. But she didn't break. Her faith in a sovereign God and a day-by-day, minute-by-minute walk with Jesus Christ gave her comfort, wisdom, and direction.

She had counseled other women over the years, "When grief and change come too fast, don't react right away. Take some time. Pray about it and let the Lord lead you." Mom recalled some advice she'd heard and passed on to others. "When you lose your husband, don't make any big moves for a year if you can help it."

There was only the little house, a car, and a meager Social Security check each month after all of the funeral expenses were paid. So she went back to work at the nursing home. Reva poured herself into her work. She believed it was a ministry to those elderly people as well as a job; and oh, how she loved those she served.

Almost a year to the day from when dad was buried, the phone rang in my office 300 miles away. "Thomas, I've put the house up for sale and I've reserved an apartment in a new complex where I grew up (Kansas). It's near my sisters and brothers and they need me to be near them. I already have a job in the apartment complex office." With Cheke's and my help, she was settled in a brand new apartment within a few months. Mom had come full circle. The place she lived was built on the grounds where her high school building used to stand.

She sometimes said she was lonely and missed dad terribly, but mom was pleased to know that her husband was seeing the Lord face-to-face. And with that she dedicated herself to serving the Lord in her church, working beyond the call of duty in her job, and reaching out to one of her brothers and one of her sisters that really needed help.

Over the ensuing years, Mom and I had many spiritual, philosophical, and personal encounters with each other. I remember well the discussions about how she responded to the many changes in her life and how she actually instigated some of those changes. I'll never forget our conversation one evening on her apartment balcony. "Thomas, life has been tough, but the memories are so special. Many of the changes weren't the way I wanted them to happen. But the way I look at it, and what I see in so many people through out my life, a person has two choices. One is to fight those changes that they don't like and can't do anything about and become bitter. The bitterness eats on them like cancer. Believe me. Those people aren't fun to be around. The other is to recognize that God has His hand in it and try to find something to take delight in about the change. At least those people are worth having over for dessert."

Fast-forward a few years; Reva is in her 80s. Still working and up to her elbows in her church. And then they got a new young pastor. Now that was a change. He was an okay preacher, and he and his wife sang great duets. But he put a screen next to the pulpit and used one of those projector things. Besides showing an outline of his sermon as he preached (mom liked that because many years earlier she had been a teacher), he put the words to songs up there for people to sing. Called them Praise Songs. He didn't even use the hymnal. When they called (hired) him, they had no idea that he played the guitar. The organist and pianist didn't like it much. They weren't needed except to play the prelude and offertory.

Reva watched for a few Sundays and then called me. After listening to her frustrations, I asked, "Mom, what have you done about it?" Then she really unloaded, "I'm about to raise some issues with the deacons—at least bring it up at the next ladies meeting. We didn't ask for this!"

"Mom, have you prayed out it? Have you seen any new kinds of results from this? Are you going to become one of those bitter people that aren't any fun to be around? Cool it for awhile and call me back in a few weeks after you've prayed about it. But don't change your personality at your age. You're too special the way you are."

The call came about a month later. "Thomas! Guess what's happened at church. We have a van picking up under-privileged kids from a town nearby and attendance is growing. Besides, it isn't just us old folks anymore. There are young families showing up. I don't think they give very much in the offering plate because they don't have much. So I'll just give more. The change is so great. God is so good. I'll never learn those songs like the old hymns, but the kids really sing out now. The few we had before didn't even open their mouths."

Fast-forward to year 86 for Reva. My phone rang again. "It's time for a change. Do you want my car or should I sell it and send you the money?" "Mom, what happened?" "Nothing! I just think that I'm too old to drive anymore—a real hazard on the road and I don't want to hurt anyone." "But how will you get to the store and to church?" "There is a van that goes to the store every Tuesday, and friends have offered to take me to church anytime I want to go. And, if I don't want to cook, the van goes to the Senior Citizen's Center every day for lunch."

Over the next two years, Reva lost momentum. She had given up her job at 85, her car at 86, and was getting confused more and more. I arranged for help to stop by each day, but that didn't seem to provide the kind of care that mom needed. One night about 9:30, my phone rang once more. "Thomas, I'm too confused to get myself into bed. I think I need help." "Mom, can you make it until morning? I'll come right away but the drive is 600 miles and I can't get there until tomorrow night."

"Oh, that's all right. I'll sit up and watch TV until morning if I have to." At 7:45 the next morning, my phone rang again. It was the social worker at the nearby hospital near mom's apartment. "Your mom checked in here last night about 10:30. A neighbor friend brought her. Reva said she was confused and ready for a nursing home. You know what, we think she's right. We'll help you make all the arrangements if you'll give us direction."

"I'll be there in a few hours. In the meantime, call Chapman Valley Manor and make sure they have a room."

I spent last weekend with mom and took her to church on Sunday. Standing beside me, she sang both the hymns and the Praise Songs. She carries a pretty good tune for a 90 year old. After we had Sunday dinner at a restaurant she used to like, she told me,

> "This food isn't nearly as good as it is at Chapman Valley Manor. That is the finest resort I could have ever hoped to live in. They take care of everything for me. All I need to do is help people with their bibs and get them back to the right rooms. The Lord sure is good. The changes have all been a delight. I just wish God would hurry up and make the final change for me. I want to see Him face-to-face."

Did Reva navigate her change mazes successfully? How do you define "success" when doing a post mortem review of changes you've navigated (or are stuck in)?

Recognizing and experiencing delight in change is a matter of a person's will. And the will that is controlled by the facts (mind) and emotions (heart) often takes the bitter route that Reva talked about. Figure 12.1 illustrates the spectrum of responses to changes that you may think you can't control.

CHANGE-REACTION SCALE

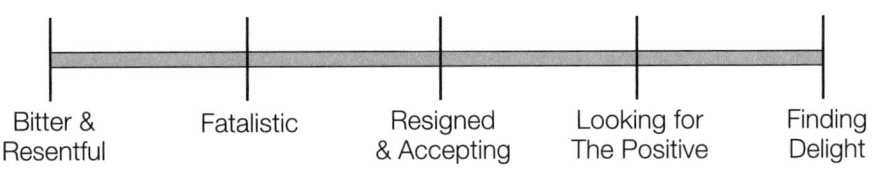

Bitter & Resentful | Fatalistic | Resigned & Accepting | Looking for The Positive | Finding Delight

FIGURE 12.1

Sometimes when high momentum, blind-side changes hit, a person's first emotion is to be Bitter & Resentful. But as Reva's life demonstrated, her Christ-centeredness moved her to acknowledge the facts (her husband died) and experience the emotions (grief), but she ended up by finding delight through her faith. An emotionally healthy person generally moves along the Change-

Reaction Scale from left to right; even if the change is so traumatic that their initial response is way over on the left. And some people walk so close to the Lord that no matter what happens, they always operate on the right.

Here are a few reality examples that illustrate the Change-Reaction Scale.

Reacting to Change

MINI-CASE 1

Rudy worked hard but he was not prepared for the kind of work he was asked to do. His skills were exceptional—just not related to his assignment. The department didn't need what he could contribute. Finally, after several attempts to retrain and help Rudy, I was forced to release him. Rudy's reaction was to want to sue me and the company; but fortunately he didn't act on that impulse.

Six months later, Rudy asked to meet with me. Although I was afraid of disgruntled employee violence, I agreed. Rudy sat in my office and gave this perspective: "Tom, getting fired from this company was the best thing that ever happened to me. I took your counsel. I looked for a job that used my talents and skills and interests, too. I found that kind of job. My new boss likes my work, I enjoy going to work, and my family has seen a change in me that they can't believe. Thanks for forcing me to change."

MINI-CASE 2

Pastor Henderson had years of success in a small church. The Lord blessed his work as he ministered caringly to the seniors who represented about 70 percent of the congregation. Then we called him to be our senior pastor. Our church was considerably larger and had very different demographics: younger families, doctors and executives, several associate pastors. After several years, we elders realized that Pastor Hendersen was over his head in leading the church staff and ministering to the family and professional needs of the majority of the flock. Sermons were good-to-excellent Sunday after Sunday, but his pastoring and leadership styles were ineffective.

We met night after night to pray about the situation, about Pastor Hendersen and his ministry, and about our own attitudes. Finally we made a tough decision and, in love, approached Pastor Hendersen with a plan to help him find a new ministry within a year. His immediate reaction was one of anger: "How dare you release me. God called me to be the Senior Pastor in this church and here's where I'll stay."

As a result, the church was asked to vote whether Pastor Hendersen should stay or leave. He used every method of persuasion he could think of, but the vote was 92 percent that he leave. To this day he is filled with bitterness and continues to criticize the church and its members.

MINI-CASE 3

Cheke and I moved to a quiet, growing, and restful rural community in the South. Our business required me to travel about two weeks each month, and I could run the rest of the business by phone and the Internet. We were able to enjoy the warmer weather and the countryside. The nearest town, 13 miles away, was past its prime but provided a post office, court house, churches, and the necessities of life.

Within a mile of our new community, there were a few relaxed restaurants, a bank, a convenience store with gas pumps, and one forgiving golf course with another on the way. A lake nearby added to the serenity and relaxation.

And then the place began to change. It was relentless. The community expanded to four golf courses (actually seven if you count the adjoining developments). A 5-star convention hotel was built in our development. A top drawer grocery store along with strip malls for shopping sprang up. Those relaxed restaurants hired foreign chefs and required long pants and jackets. A golf school and fitness center and top notch marina were added. Land prices and home prices went through the roof. Several churches were built and filled with people each week. At the same time, that town 13 miles north imploded as businesses began to move out to the lake area, leaving empty buildings behind.

Cheke was less than excited about the changes. Her attitude was that we moved to this setting to get away from such a fast pace and to let up a bit. But she was resigned herself to the fact that change is inevitable, and she was delighted to see people get involved in the new churches.

As for me, I was thrilled. I didn't see it as change as much as progress. Growth brings excitement and to not change means that decay and death are right around the corner—as it was for the town 13 miles away.

MINI-CASE 4

I walked into Katherine's office as she was hanging up the phone. We hadn't seen each other for a few months and I stopped by to check on her. "How's your family doing? What's happening with those boys of yours?" Then I realized that Katherine seemed a bit shaken. Tears welled in her eyes and started to run down her cheeks. I couldn't tell if she was hurt or bitter or upset.

"Our oldest, Andrew, is in the Marines and he's in Iraq—Fallujah where the fighting is. And Mark will be shipping out for Iraq in a few days. He's a Marine, too." All I could do was try to comfort her and promise her that I'd continue to pray for them.

And then she stopped. "And my baby, Tim—I just hung up the phone after talking with him when you walked in. He's a senior in high school and called to tell me that he had just finished meeting with a Marine recruiter. He's signed up to enlist as soon as he graduates."

Then the sweetest and calmest smile crossed her face. The tears seemed to dry by themselves. "Tom, I'm so proud of those boys I could burst. Imagine, if they are killed, they will have died for a worthy cause—freedom. They were brought up to trust God and all three believe this is what He wants them to do. It sure would be better than running into a tree or having some other accident and dying for no good reason at all."

People in these four cases were at different places along the Change-Reaction Scale. And usually, after thinking about it, they shifted to the right on the scale. They moved from cope to hope. Except for Pastor Hendersen; his bitterness ate him up and not only impacted his own life, but also his reputation and the lives of those around him.

What's the foundation for moving from bitterness to delight? Scripture speaks plainly about the subject.

> See to it that no one comes short of the grace of God; that no root of bitterness springing up causes trouble, and by it many be defiled.
> Hebrews 12:15

The saddest characteristic about bitterness is that it destroys you from the inside and then destroys those around you. But even more troubling is the fact that it saddens our Lord.

At the other end of the scale is Delight in Change. A person who is Christ-centered has no guarantee of only facing change labyrinths that please. In fact, God may decide that one of His children should face more severe changes than most people do. His purposes are rarely understood. But the ability of the Christ-follower to move quickly from cope to hope is based on another encouragement from the Lord.

> Rejoice always; pray without ceasing; in everything give thanks; for this is God's will for you in Christ Jesus. I Thessalonians 5:16-18

> And we know that God causes all things to work together for good to those who love God, to those who are called according to His purpose. Romans 8:28

You probably know yourself better than anyone else knows you. If you can, for a moment, imagine yourself when you're not confronted with a major change maze. Where do you think you normally fit on the Change Capacity Spectrum (resistor, slow follower, fast follower, new idea person)? And where do you usually start on the Change Reaction Scale? How do you think you should move on both scales as your relationship with Jesus Christ grows?

CHAPTER THIRTEEN
The Spiritual Perspective

Have you ever faced a change or become stuck in a change maze or emerged from the maze wondering, "What was that all about? Why did that change happen to me?" As you have tried to learn from the experience, have you played the tape back by rehashing the facts and reliving the emotions only to come up with no answers?

We often find it difficult to accept a change experience, especially if it is a troublesome labyrinth, because we limit our perspective to the mind and heart dimensions. But we might find some answers, insights, and comfort if we look at it from the third dimension of the soul. Remember, this dimension focuses on the spiritual, eternal, Christ-centered view.

You probably know people who walk with Christ each day. They talk with Him in prayer and dig into His Word as part of their way of life. These people give of their resources and energy to His work out of love for their Lord. And yet they are bombarded by change after change after change. Maybe you're one of those people that others just shake their heads about and wonder, "What did you do to deserve all of that?"

It may not be much consolation, but the Bible is full of examples where God-following, Christ-centered believers encountered a barrage of change mazes. To name a few, Abraham was asked of God to change from being a wealthy farmer to living as a wandering nomad. Joseph was changed from a darling son to a slave and later to a leader. Moses changed from enjoying all of the perks of an adopted son of the Egyptian king to serving as the leader of a rebellious horde of people traveling through the desert. Ruth lost both her husband and father-in-law on the way to becoming the great grandmother of David and an ancestor of Jesus. David was changed from a shepherd boy to a king. Nehemiah was changed from a cup bearer to a leader. Elizabeth was changed from a barren, elderly woman into the mother of John the Baptist. Peter was changed from a fisherman to a church leader. Paul was changed from a persecutor of Christians to an Apostle of Christ. And the list goes on.

But you can look at those examples and argue that it's plain to see that God was using those pillars of the faith to further His kingdom. What about the barrage of change mazes that you encounter that yank you around and thwart your agenda for no apparent reason?

Recognize that most of those biblical people didn't know at the time what God was using those changes for. In fact, many of them never learned in their life-time what the purposes were for the changes in their lives. Do you think that Paul, when he wrote letters to churches and Christian friends, imagined that those same letters would teach and admonish and encourage us today? Think about it! God threw gigantic labyrinths into his life like putting him in prison and wrecking some of the ships he was on so that he'd have time to write.

I can't build a list of reasons why God puts changes in your life. I can't even build a complete list for my life. But by recalling and examining many of the changes that God has sent my way, I have observed a few absolute truths that apply in these situations. They could help make the spiritual dimension dominant over facts and emotions in changes in your life.

ABSOLUTES

1. God has purpose in everything to bring Glory to Himself.

2. God loves you and takes your best interest to heart.

3. God's view of best interest is always focused on the eternal life perspective.

4. God planned and knows your future (for all eternity).

5. God sacrificed His Son, Jesus, in order to offer you a future with Him.

6. God is willing to have you sacrifice your earthly well-being to further His work.

7. God is the source of comfort and solace when the mazes overwhelm you.

8. God surrounds you with spiritual brothers and sisters to help and encourage you.

9. God builds, changes, solves, and removes change mazes in your life to get and keep you on His agenda.

10. God's plan is for you to grow to be more like Him throughout your lifetime.

TABLE 13.1

If you took the time to think about it, you could add more absolutes from your life. That list can become another tool for your navigation kit. Look more closely at the last one: God's plan is for you to grow to be more like Him throughout your lifetime.

If you go back to figure 4.3 in Chapter 4, you'll recall that your mind will stop thinking and your heart will stop beating, but your soul will live through all of eternity. It is critical that you remember and dwell on the fact that God uses all kinds of methods to grow you, a Christ-follower, to be more like Christ throughout your physical life. One of His growing/learning methods is to take you through countless changes.

A pastor of ours, Ken Abrahamson, opened my eyes to Scripture that presents the spiritual life-cycle of changes that grow us ever closer to becoming like Christ.

> I am writing to you, little children, because your sins have been forgiven you for His name's sake. I am writing to you, fathers, because you know Him who has been from the beginning. I am writing to you, young men, because you have overcome the evil one. I John 2:12-13a

It shouldn't surprise you that God uses the life-cycle to move us along spiritually just as He ordained it for physical maturing. John isn't referring to physical growth. When you received Christ, God started you all over with a new birth. And that change anchors you as one of His children. The result of moving into that change maze is that your sins are forgiven.

Then as you grow, He builds within you an ever-deepening appreciation of who God is, how He works, and what He does. You begin to realize that this is a change maze you'll never exit in this lifetime. You'll increasingly grasp the spiritual truth that God always has been and always will be; you know Him who has been from the beginning.

The next stage is where you have matured beyond being born again and you continue deepening your understanding of Him. Verse 14 goes on to say, "I have written to you, young men, because you are strong and the word of God abides in you, and you have overcome the evil one."

This says that God is equipping you to deal with, confront, enter, overcome, and emerge from any change labyrinth that Satan can throw at you. Remember Job? When he emerged from those terrible labyrinth experiences, Job delighted God even more and lived in personal rest. If you read the account in the Scriptures carefully, you'll see that God allowed Satan to throw many changes at him. Moving into the maturing stage means that you are stronger, the word of God abides in you, and you have overcome Satan.

How does God accomplish all this with the Christ-follower? It isn't a single event that turns you from a babe in Christ to a strong overcomer. It takes time. Spiritual maturing is a process that never stops. It moves well beyond continual change. One of our former pastors, Jimmy Long, signs his correspondence, Be Transformed! And our senior pastor, Dan Werthman, continually emphasizes that the walk to become more like Christ involves transformation, not just change.

Transformation is more than a change. When you are being transformed, you are moving beyond the mechanics of reacting to change mazes and labyrinths. Instead, God works in you and through you to respond to the changes you encounter. If you focus on the fact that all the mazes and labyrinths that come your way are ordained by God, you'll realize that He is using them according to His plan for you and for your spiritual maturing. That fact and the absolutes listed a few pages back should encourage you through any kind of change.

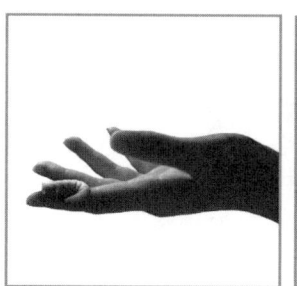

Things as they are may be moving slowly and look pretty ugly

and the process of change may be confusing and look even uglier

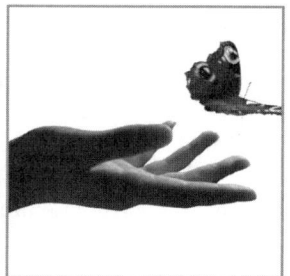

but the results can bring delight & beauty well worth the effort!

Have you ever heard the statement, "God isn't finished with me yet"? It is sometimes tiring to think that He is constantly tuning and growing and changing and improving and maturing you with every breath you take. But it is also reassuring to know, "It is God who is at work in you, both to will and to work for His good pleasure." Philippians 2:13.

A few days ago, I was walking around our yard trying to figure out a way to express the fact that God is continually transforming us to be like His Son. God gave me one of those delightful encounters with our neighbor lady, Vivian, who was working in her flower garden.

She is quite a lady. Viv spent most of her life on a farm in the Red River Valley of North Dakota. Christ flows from her with every action and every word. Her life is a walking testimony of God's grace.

Her husband, another Christ-follower, died about 10 years ago from a lengthy and painful disease. As we talked about the fact that God is transforming us each day to become more like Him, she related that He had taught her much and cared for her well over the years. Many of the changes have been really tough, but she gets excited about each day because God is working to help her to become more like Christ.

Then she told me more about her husband, Orrie, his illness, and his death. She beamed when she told me about being able to see visible transformation in Orrie's life during his illness and right up to his death. Viv described the last change she saw God do in his life.

Orrie was a fighter. He loved life and when he became ill, he fought it with vigor. Her view of the whole change labyrinth is worth noting. In her words, "They were terrible yet glorious changes; the suffering, the resistance, and then the submitting and the peace. I watched this man be transformed before my very eyes. He truly became all that God planned for him to be. Orrie changed from looking back to looking ahead. People would come to visit my husband in the hospital. And what did he do? He'd ask them if he could pray for them instead of them praying for him." He went to be with the Lord with great excitement and anticipation about seeing Christ face-to-face."

The added dimension of a Christ-guided perspective takes your focus away from the facts and the emotions. He changes your journey through the labyrinth's high walls and narrow corridors into an adventure that helps you to become more like Christ.

FIGURE 13.2

God superimposes His spiritual growth plan for us on change labyrinths to make us more like Christ. As He says in Jeremiah 18:6, "Behold like the clay in a potter's hand, so are you in My hand."

Section 4 Chapters 12 & 13 PonderPoints

1. Think about one of the significant changes you recently experienced or are experiencing now. It could be one that you decided to initiate (like taking a new job or enrolling in a new course or getting engaged or . . .) or one that blindsided you unexpectedly. It may be one that you welcomed or one that is giving you grief. Briefly describe it.

2. For the change you described, place a ✓ in one of the three dimension columns that is most appropriate for each item. No multiple ✓s allowed!

ITEM	FACTS	EMOTIONS	FAITH
What initially told you that you were confronted with a change?			
What influenced you the most when you first encountered the change maze?			
What dominated your approach as you tried to wind your way through the maze?			
What was the most difficult dimension while navigating the change?			

3. Place an X at the place on the Change-Reaction Scale where you think you normally land when you're

first confronted with change. Then based on Chapter 13 ("The Spiritual Perspective"), what should be your target as you grow to be more Christ-like? Mark the place with a T.

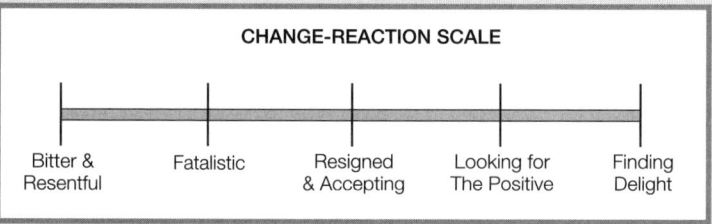

4. What absolutes from Table 13.1 do you think will help you move from X to T on the Change-Reaction Scale?

5. From your own experiences in your Christ-centered walk, what other absolutes can you add to strengthen your Change Maze Navigation Kit?

6. Jeremiah 18:4 says, But the vessel that he was making of clay was spoiled in the hand of the potter; so he remade it into another vessel, as it pleased the potter to make.

Ponder what that says to you about the change mazes and labyrinths you encounter in your life. Which dimension is dominant? Who is in control of your change mazes and your way of navigating"?

SECTION 5

WHAT IF YOU'RE CALLED
to lead change?

Until now this book has focused on the characteristics of change, how change impacts you, how you deal with change, and the results of change. But what if you want to affect change? What if you want to make change happen? Or what if you're a new-idea person who wants to be a difference maker? What if you're called of God to lead change (even if you don't want to or don't feel adequate)?

This book isn't about leadership per se, but the topic can't be completely ignored when we talk about leading change. There is continual debate about whether leaders are born with the innate aptitude to lead or whether people can be trained to be leaders. We aren't going to get into that controversy here. Instead let's look at a leader as someone called of God, either from birth or through training, but in either case spiritually gifted for the task.

Here is a quick summary of characteristics of a leader that I discovered when asked to do a study of prominent business leaders across the country. That study resulted in the development of a mentoring and consulting approach that

I use called The Marks of Leadership[7], Some of those marks can't be ignored when you are called to lead change.

A GOOD LEADER

1	Respects others
2	Finds value in all people
3	Is called to lead and willing to follow
4	Is able and willing to communicate
5	Withstands pressure and stress
6	Knows when to persist and when to change
7	Is willing to stand alone
8	Takes personal risk to reduce the risk to others
9	Provides meaningful vision
10	Establishes clear direction

Selected From *The Marks of Leadership*

Two aspects of leading change are examined in this section: 1) Situations in which you're asked or assigned to lead a group of people to carry out a change, and 2) Situations in which you sense that God is calling you to become a difference maker by instigating and driving a change, with or without the help of other people.

[7] LGI Executive Briefing Paper

CHAPTER FOURTEEN
Making Change

When considering people who lead change, we often think of the New Idea People shown on the Change Capacities graph (Chapter 2). But that isn't always the case. There could be times in your life when you are pressed into leading change—even when it isn't your idea or you don't have the innate ability. Circumstances and/or a situation and/or a passion can cause a person to take on the role regardless. I have a good friend who didn't necessarily consider himself a leader and shied away from being one. But when he recognized the election corruption in the county, his passion for ethics and fairness drove him to step forward to lead a group to clean it up. And they succeeded in just a few years of hard and focused effort.

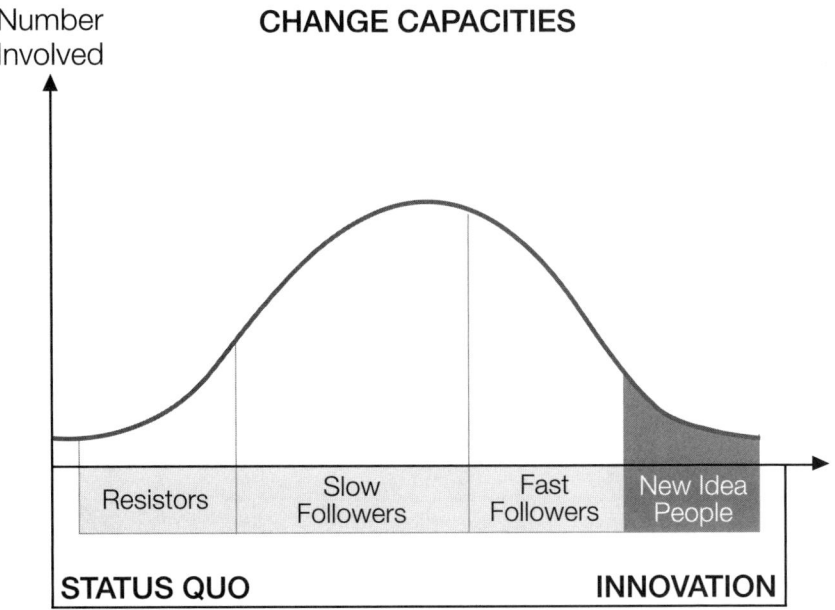

FIGURE 14.1

With that said, a study of organizations in general (business, government, church, universities, families, sports teams, etc.) reveals that most innovation and ideas for change come from just a few people. The rest of the team falls into the three left-most categories.

The role and life of a new idea person is often miserable and unrewarding because as they are driven to introduce change, resistance rises. History is filled with examples of people who have tried to make a difference and met with ongoing resistance: Jesus, Paul, Attila the Hun, Churchill, Augustine, Luther, Jonathan Edwards, Calvin, Lincoln, Susan B. Anthony, Amelia Earhart, Martin Luther King, Jr., Darwin, John & Charles Wesley, and the list goes on.

Bringing about meaningful change requires work. Obviously the more dramatic the change, the more the effort required to make it happen. And the law of inertia can be applied to change just like physics: "For every action there is an equal and opposite reaction." In change language, that says that for every change force there is a resistance force. And the stronger the change, the stronger the resistance.

In previous chapters, we looked at the kinds of change and how they impacted the individual. The following table displays some of the change issues that combine to define a change force.

MAGNITUDE	SPEED	TYPE
High	Fast	Traumatic
Medium	Average	Sporadic
Low	Slow	Predictable

TABLE 14.2

There are certainly more combinations than those shown here. But it doesn't require too much reasoning to recognize that a change that is high/fast/traumatic will create stronger resistance than a change that is low/slow/predictable.

If you want to introduce change, it is worthwhile to evaluate both the change force required and the resistance force it will create. Remember the steps toward hitting the wall? The first six steps can also be used to describe the resistance steps that will be generated as the change intensity increases. The following three figures are examples of what to expect in resistance force depending on the change force.

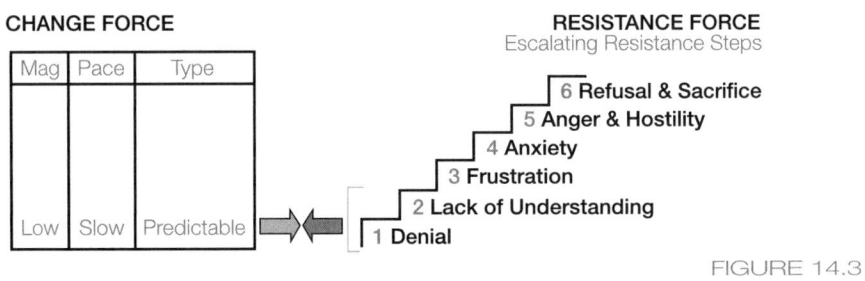

FIGURE 14.3

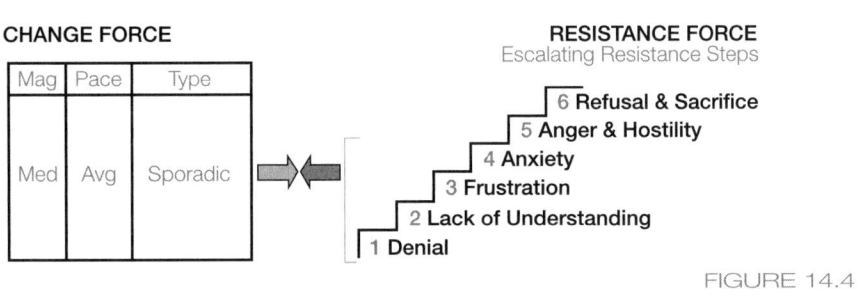

FIGURE 14.4

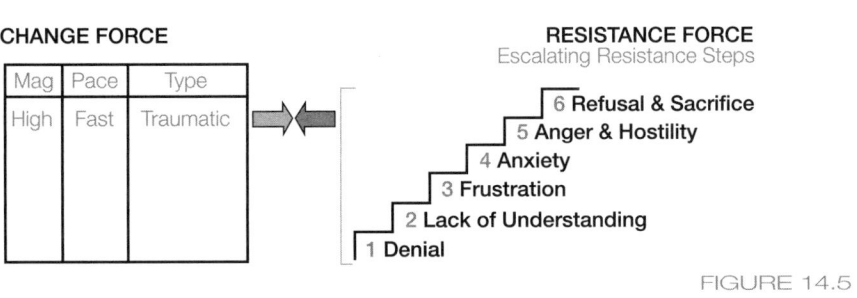

FIGURE 14.5

Notice—not only does the resistance force climb the steps as the change force intensifies, but each new resistance step includes the previous steps. So when the change is high/fast/traumatic, all of the resistance steps are at work to push back and resist.

Table 14.6 shows some of the ways resistance manifests itself. The more intense the change, the more of these actions are brought to bear in building resistance.

RESISTANCE STEPS	RESISTANCE ACTIONS
Denial	Refuses to acknowledge that the change is happening; refuses to acknowledge that the change is necessary; ignores the change
Lack of Understanding	Doesn't understand the change or why it is happening; uses "I don't understand" to confound the change; pleads ignorance and won't participate
Frustration	Continually pleads that the change is frustrating and, therefore, must be stopped; is not always logical in expressing resistance; may add non-related issues to the change issue
Anxiety	Frets and worries to the point of sometimes getting physically and/or emotionally ill; may use the illness to try to force the change to stop; begins to erode the spiritual view
Anger & Hostility	Expresses irrational thinking and acts out anger; threatens physical and/or verbal hostile actions; may carry out those hostile resistance actions; tries to bring non-related issues and people to confound the change; allows emotions to take over and facts to become distorted
Refusal & (Self) Sacrifice	Refuses to go along with the change; holds a sit-down strike; won't abide by the change; is willing to sacrifice personal reputation and sometimes physical well being to resist the change; sacrifices personal values, ethics, and basic beliefs in carrying out verbal and physical acts of resistance; sacrifices facts and spiritual principles for emotions control

TABLE 14.6

Before looking at steps that can be taken to overcome the resistance, let's link with another concept that complicates the change process even further. Remember the discussion of Culture, Structure, & Life issues in Chapter 2? An individual's situation as it relates to those issues at the time the change hits has a significant impact on how quickly and how high they will escalate up the Resistance Steps.

Think about it! Imagine a person who is absolutely anchored in his family and/or church and/or geography and/or age and/or ethnicity and/or traditional culture, and he is pleased with the surrounding structure of his everyday activities. And further imagine that this person feels that his physical or financial or comfortable well-being (life) is threatened by a change that alters any or all of those issues. Such a person won't slowly ascend the resistance steps. He'll bound up the stairs three at a time—unless he is dominated by his faith and has a Christ-Centered view of today and eternity. Note: Being a Christ-follower does not mean that a person will not resist a change that is counter to his beliefs. It does mean that the person will be prayerful, rational, and respectful in the way he resists.

So, if you're called to bring about change—how is it done? There are a few fundamental actions that could help you lead others into a change maze and at least reduce the resistance. (Very seldom does a major change happen where resistance doesn't surface. Get used to resistance if you're leading change or a difference maker.)

1 Really think through the details of the change. Put together a meaningful description of the AS-IS (the way things are now). Then list reasons why the change is needed. Detail the TO-BE (how things will look after the change has happened). Note: The further up the change chart (Table 14.2), the more detailed this should be before introducing the change.

2 Determine the real timetable whereby the change must be accomplished.

3 Identify those people who will be impacted by the change and determine their most-likely category: resister, slow follower, or fast follower. See Figure 14.1. (Remember, you're probably a new idea person. At least you are pushing for the change.)

4 Then identify the people most affected by the change—both for good or for bad. Determine where those people are (as individuals and as a group) on all of the structure, culture, and life issues. Identify those people who might take on a role of leading the resistance and those who could help with making the change.

5 With the information about the details of the change and a good understanding of the people who will be impacted, build a strategy to inform and sell the concepts of the change. You might include the following action steps:

   a Telegraph the ideas surrounding the change, in advance of formal discussions, with those who can be most helpful in making it happen (the people you'll have to lead).

   b Form small-interest groups—around each of the three change dimensions—to examine the AS-IS and explain the need for change. (This may start to generate resistance, but don't change direction—just listen and log ideas and points of contention.)

   c Begin to discuss the values/benefits of a suggested TO-BE.

   d In the small-interest groups, surface some of the alternative approaches to reaching the change objective (TO-BE).

   e Communicate with the entire group of people who will be directly impacted by the change (where possible) about the AS-IS, TO-BE, reasons and benefits of the change, how you plan to carry it out, and an estimate of the timetable.

6 Monitor the resistance carefully and be prepared to abandon the hard-core resistors in order to concentrate on the slow followers and fast followers.

7 Begin to involve the fast followers and slow followers in carrying out the change. Make them a part of it and recognize their value in achieving the benefits of the change.

8 Monitor the risk of failure by watching six things.

  a After the change, will the anticipated results happen no matter how difficult the change?

  b Are you able to withstand the resistance personally and willing to stay the course? Is it worth the price?

  c Are you continuing to pursue the change as a matter of pride and principle or is it truly valuable?

  d Has the value/benefit of the change continued to be the focus or has the adventure of the change become the objective?

  e Are you willing to abandon the hard-core resistors and really move on without them or are you intending to compromise in a way that keeps them around? (If you do, you can expect them to fight a guerrilla action against the change sometime in the future.)

  f Monitor to make sure that the facts and the emotions are not replacing the eternal values!

9 Continue to communicate progress of the change and reasons for shifts in progress, and always focus on the TO-BE that will happen when the change is in place.

10 When the change (or a specific phase, if it is a multi-phase change) has occurred, celebrate the event and look forward to the forecasted results.

11 Be sure to include the slow followers, fast followers, and converted resistors in the celebration.

12 In almost all cases, more change will be necessary because you have learned more, can now see further toward the horizon of the benefits, and know the cost of making the change. Be prepared to move on quickly.

Think of it this way. You know what it is like to encounter change mazes and labyrinths. Hopefully you've learned to pursue the soul dimension early in the process so that the Lord can help you navigate through them.

Now you're called to lead a change, and let's assume it's complex enough that it takes the form of a labyrinth. You've examined navigation principles and fundamentals presented earlier in this book to help you form thoughtful processes as you move into change labyrinths. Remember how you struggled with risk, uncertainty, and rate? Remember what it was like to look for God's leadership as you moved ahead?

Put yourself in the shoes of those you are leading. They may have all of the misgivings about change that you've experienced and may not want to venture into the maze. They may not be Christ-followers and, therefore, not have the assurances you have with Him as your pilot and His Word as a navigation tool. As their leader, it's up to you to demonstrate that you do have access to a Guide and to tools that cover all three dimensions. Realize that the change labyrinth you're entering will probably lead to a lot of changes for each of them.

FIGURE 14.7

High/fast/traumatic change is not without significant cost. The resistance will never stop entirely. And in some cases, when resistors reach steps 5 and 6 (anger & hostility and refusal & self-sacrifice), much of the support you thought you had will vanish. If you are led by the Lord and are Christ-Centered to the point that you are at peace with what you are doing and where you are going, stay the course. But if you begin to doubt His direction, take a checkpoint to make sure it is the Lord's will, not your own.

> For it is God who is at work in you both to will and to work for *His* good pleasure. Philippians 2:13

CHAPTER FIFTEEN
Role of a Difference Maker

If you think that being the target of change is traumatic, try being the person on the bleeding edge of making a sudden, far-reaching, radical change. The role of a difference maker can be lonely, difficult, harsh, sleepless, challenging, debilitating, fatiguing, threatening, and even worse.

So why do it? If you sense that you are called to take on the leadership role in regard to a particular change, or if you see eternal spiritual tragedy for someone, or if the realities of the AS-IS are fatal for those around you, then no matter the price, you must become a difference maker. Look at the passion and sacrifice of Jesus Christ and the reason He did it. Read the New Testament to learn why and how, and the price paid by Paul to be a dynamic, relentless, never-tiring, fearless, change agent for the good news of Eternal Life.

And if the change is done with spiritual peace because Christ is at the center and it is done well, then the delight of making it happen is worth it all.

In the RealityCase "Just a Sling and a Few Stones," change was high/fast/traumatic and full of serious risk. The resistance was strong and backed by tradition. The resisters were relentless. As you read the case, make note of how many of the Change Actions described at the end of Chapter 14 apply.

 RealityCase

Just a Sling and a Few Stones

The fraternities and sororities had dominated the homecoming festivity, called Shout, at Brazos University since the whole thing began. Shout was supposed to be a school-wide talent contest that gave everyone an opportunity to put together a musical or dramatic event that—after getting past the qualifying judges—would be performed night after night during homecoming week. It was designed to get the student body involved in putting on high-quality entertainment for the alumni who returned to Brazos for the festive occasion as well as attract thousands from surrounding communities.

Then, on the final night of the festivities, awards were presented for the best performances throughout the week. Categories included originality, musical excellence (both vocal and instrumental), choreography, drama, acting, and scripting, But the ultimate award was to be selected to perform at Bearskin in the spring in front of some of the country's top talent scouts. Over the years, some Shout/Bearskin performers had turned into nationally recognized performers.

As you might suspect, the selection, planning, preparation, competitiveness—and financial investment—involved in putting together the various performances got pretty intense. It came to the point where the competition between fraternities and sororities became fierce. These social organizations—especially those with big bucks and backed by wealthy alumni and parents—would hire choreographers from Broadway or Hollywood to design the acts. As much as $10,000 would be spent on getting professional coaching, and the planning would begin as least a year ahead of the performance.

The university administrators had mixed thoughts on the whole process. On the one hand, it was a tradition that could not be stopped and next to the football game was the highlight of homecoming week. Besides, it brought in lots of dollars from ticket sales to fund extra-curricular programs across Brazos. On the other hand, the whole thing was now under the control of the well-to-do, the fraternities and sororities, and the elite on campus. The average student didn't have a chance of being involved. In a way, Shout was out of control.

The faculty and the administration—and even the Board of Trustees—got involved! Many had been members of fraternities or sororities—and many were now sponsors. So they got involved in a personal way.

Oh, there were rules. Like the one that said expenses had to be limited to $1,000. But just like in college sports, there were ways around that. Alumni would send specialists to help out—and pay the bills directly so the money never passed through the organizations' books. And the rules said that any group on campus could enter—groups such as the Baptist Student Union or the Student Hospital Auxiliary—but there was absolutely no way those kids could compete. Besides, some pretty entrenched faculty and administrators made up the committee that decided which acts would perform and which acts weren't good enough.

Realize that the whole culture said that about 75 percent of Brazos' student body couldn't be involved. And that was a sore point with many of the students. For years they had complained and tried to participate, but there was no way they could make the cut. The committee and the culture made sure of that.

In 1987, some of the students in the business school led an effort to change all of that. An experimental course was designed and offered to confront senior business students with the kinds of realities they would face in the real world. The dean asked me to make it happen because I was a seasoned businessman who had been brought into the business school to put practical content into the curriculum. "Richard, I'll do it if you give me the top 50 senior students for a 2-semester course and let me run it like a company instead of a university program." Richard liked the idea. He was looking for a devoted Christ-follower to give these students some street-smarts and teach them how to deal with the real world without compromising their faith.

The course was named ACCEL, standing for Accelerated Change, Communication, Ethics, and Leadership. (Soon the students involved just called it Street Smart.) One of the services the company offered was consulting. And one of their first assignments was to conduct a study of the processes and traditions at Brazos that were hindering its growth and effectiveness (not a popular assignment with the president and most of the administration or the faculty, but really liked by the students). Within about a week, several aggressive students zeroed in on the whole Shout tradition. They quickly presented a preliminary report to the rest of ACCEL. It covered a number of problems including a breach of ethics (in the way acts were selected), bypassing Shout rules, bias in the way it was run to favor fraternities and sororities, and misuse of funds.

With one of the students facilitating the company-wide discussion, they explored ways to change the whole process. (Remember, none of these students had any real authority at Brazos.) Then one of the sharp young ladies in the class came up with a suggestion: "Why don't we put together an act ourselves and try to enter it. If they stop us, we have a case—and if they don't, we've started to change the process and the tradition. We only have six weeks before homecoming and the frats and sororities have been planning and practicing for a year, but what do you think?"

Let me explain some of the dynamics of the class. There were kids in ACCEL who belonged to fraternities and sororities who were actually in Shout events already. But as the emerging leaders of the class pleaded their case, stressing that Brazos needed to make some dramatic changes and right some wrongs, even those involved in Shout through other groups became supportive.

Well, how do you lead a change in an organization that is very comfortable with things as they are? Here are some of the things the students did.

1. They obtained a copy of the published rules and decided to follow them to the letter.

2. They got faculty sponsors and submitted a formal application.

3. They surveyed many of the students, especially those that weren't members of social fraternities and sororities, and found out the kind of event they would support.

4. And they developed a plan to raise money to fund the music, orchestra, and costumes.

Then they ran into the resistance. The Committee turned them down flat, saying that they did not have time to prepare properly and it would be an embarrassment to the university. Well, that didn't slow these kids down a bit. They continued to put the act together while several of them formally asked for a hearing by Brazos' president. (He didn't want to make any changes—so he said he was too busy.) That response hit the campus newspaper. Many of the student body let the administration know that they wanted ACCEL to have a hearing.

You guessed it. Brazos' president agreed to listen to the request and approved it. Now the act had to pass the screening process. Again it was turned down. But by this time the group studying the rules was ready. They pointed out that the ACCEL event had been screened against the standards used for the sororities and fraternities; there was another category of standards that was on the books, though it had never actually been used. Sure enough, with some strong and well-prepared presentations to administrators and the committee, it was approved.

Then came the real coupe! The students found out that organizations having no source of funds—and ACCEL didn't—were eligible to receive $500 from the university to participate in Shout. The frats had used it for years even though they had resources—and now the committee had to provide funds to ACCEL.

In the meantime, the act—written by the ACCEL team using good popular music as background—came together. On the first night, the auditorium went wild! And each night they played to ovation after ovation. To be fair, it wasn't as good musically or dramatically or as well choreographed as those that had been planned and prepared for a year and were heavily funded. The judges were right that last night when ACCEL didn't win any of the formal awards. But the judges—some from out of state and really unbiased—came up with a significant decision. The ACCEL act was awarded "Best Loved by the Audience" and asked to participate in Bearskin in the spring.

But ACCEL wasn't through. After their moral and recognized success, they went after the Shout process and traditions! They all agreed that Shout was an integral part of Brazos and needed to continue. But the emphasis on money, the exclusivity, and the biased decisions should be changed. Within a month, Brazos' president called on ACCEL to submit a proposal for effective changes to the rules along with ways to enforce them. They were approved by the university administration.

That was almost 20 years ago—and the rules and tradition really did change. Shout now involves more than the rich, the connected, and the favored. The competition is broad-based to include both organizations and individuals that never could have had a chance before the kids in ACCEL became difference makers.

Feel called to be a difference maker? Here are few questions and suggestions to help you get on the right track.

First, should you do it?

1 What is the motive for doing it? (If it's to bring about real change, Yes. If it's for personal gain, maybe not!)

2 Have the anticipated results of the change been carefully articulated? (Remember, success is in the results of the change, not in the doing of the change.)

3 What is the cost of doing the change? How much energy will it take? (Are the results worth the investment?)

4 Has the resistance been evaluated? (How strong and how relevant are the reasons not to change?)

5 Is this change driven by spiritual values or ideas and emotions? (Eternity is worth it all. Emotions and facts may not be.)

Second, how do you avoid the land mines?

1 What are your weaknesses related to leading the change you are called to make?

2 Identify other new idea people and fast followers whose strengths compensate for your weaknesses and who share your passion for the results of the change—not for change itself. With these people, build a team with the complementary skills required to make it happen. Remember, it is the result that counts, not who gets the credit. That team must, at a minimum, have the following knowledge and skill set.

   a Clear understanding of the AS-IS

   b Clear grasp and vision of the TO-BE

   c Deep understanding of the people who will be impacted by the change

   d Ability to build the case for the change (Why is it important/necessary?)

   e Capability to build the strategy for moving from the AS-IS to the TO-BE f Common sense to articulate the cost of the change ($$$, energy, rejected resistors, time, and discouragement)

    g Someone with a clear head and a consistent focus on the spiritual dimension who will recognize when hearts and minds begin to take over

    h A communications guru who understands the mission of the change and its impact on those affected

3 Evaluate your own ability to focus, stay the course, and resolve to overcome distractions (Note: This does not mean avoiding new information that causes healthy reexamination of whether the change should go forward.)

4 Continue to monitor the change detractors—especially the strong resistors—for instances of change sabotage.

5 On a daily basis, urge every member of your team to assess whether their faith is directing their behavior and their resolve.

6 Never pass up an opportunity to communicate: listen, explain, and reiterate the reason for the change and the results it will bring.

Review the RealityCase, "Just a Sling and a Few Stones," in the light of these suggestions and questions and the actions described in the previous chapter. Recognize that risk, pain, sleeplessness, fatigue, and loneliness are all part of the cost of being a successful (in God's eyes) Difference Maker.

Section 5 Chapters 14 & 15 PonderPoints

1. Consider this table:

MAGNITUDE	SPEED	TYPE
High	Fast	Traumatic
Medium	Average	Sporadic
Low	Slow	Predictable

a. How would you classify the change brought about by hurricane Katrina that hit New Orleans and the surrounding states in 2005? (Magnitude, Speed, and Type)

b. Classify the change in gasoline prices after the hurricane.

2. Here is an opportunity to do a little role-playing. Read the following mini-case.

Crashes in the Night

Green Gables Road is a narrow curving road along the shore of a Minnesota lake. The speed limit is 30 mph. There have been two near-fatal car crashes in the last three months. As in years past, they happened on a sharp corner about a hundred yards from your place. Both accidents were after midnight and both drivers were intoxicated.

The driver of the car that rolled after hitting a stone wall ran into the woods and was apprehended when the sheriff's department brought in a helicopter and used search lights to find him. The driver of the car in the second accident took out a stone pillar, a 30 year-old apple tree, and pine trees. The car was totaled.

Out at the point, at the end of the road, is a restaurant and bar, which is the supply source for many drunk drivers—and the source of considerable tax revenue to the town and county. Repeated pleas to town councilmen to have the establishment's parking lot, exit road, and the bar itself patrolled and cited have gotten head nods with no action.

Your neighbors are getting upset. Besides all the property damage, human lives are in danger. The neighbors have asked you to lead the effort to get the situation changed so that Green Gables Road is a safe place to live and drive.

Respond to the following questions about the mini-case.

      a. Identify the fast followers.

      b. Identify the resistors.

      c. Determine what has to be changed.

      d. Determine who has to be changed.

e. What are the results you and your team want (the TO-BE)?

f. What are the facts about the AS-IS?

g. How do you convince slow followers in the neighborhood to join the effort?

h. Assess the risks to you and your neighbors if the effort fails.

i. What is your approach to a neighbor who adamantly refuses to get involved?

j. What and how would you communicate about the planned change?

k. What is the magnitude/speed/type of this change, as you see it?

3. Jesus himself gives every Christ-follower a directive to be a difference maker! In Matthew 29:19-20a, He says, "Therefore go and make disciples of all nations, baptizing them in the name of the Father and of the Son and of the Holy Spirit, and teaching them to obey everything I have commanded you."

You're being told to be a Difference Maker.

Hesitant to tell someone else about the ultimate change that Christ made within you? Think you don't have the skills to do it? Scared it will backfire? Based on your personality, where do you think you are on the Change Capacity graph?

Jesus tells you that He'll provide support in carrying out his command. "And surely I am with you always, to the very end of the age." (Matthew 28:20b).

Jesus means what He says. How does recognizing that fact impact your position on the Change Capacity graph when it comes to being a Change Agent for Christ?

summary & conclusion

Remember the three dimensions of change: mind, heart, and soul? The intent of this book has been to equip you with understanding, tools, and a way to think, so that you can navigate effectively with all three as you encounter change. When change happens in your life, how do you adapt and move through the corridors of the change maze? If you're working to make change happen, how do you attempt to get others to join you in making it a reality?

You've been exposed to change concepts that should be of value whether you're the changer or the changee. Here is a summary of key concepts to keep in mind.

FROM SECTION I

We used these terms to examine a variety of change mazes:

TERM	CHANGE CONCEPTS 101
Continuous Change	Prolonged change without interruption
Sporadic Change	Change that occurs at irregular intervals and has no pattern or order
Predictable Change	Change that can be anticipated in advance and is often inevitable
Blind-Side Change	Change that is a complete surprise; sudden
Traumatic Change	Change that causes emotional upset and may even cause physical harm
Subtle Change	Change that is so slight that it is difficult to detect or analyze
Rate of Change	The speed at which change occurs
Accelerated Change	Increasing rate of change; change that occurs sooner than expected
Magnitude of Change	The size, extent, significance, or degree of impact caused by the change
Complex Change	Change that is made up of multiple, involved, and complicated changes that happen simultaneously

TABLE 1.4

Change mazes are often thought to be only two-dimensional; however, the most effective way for you to navigate in them and through them requires you to understand the third dimension.

FIRST DIMENSION:
Mind = facts, system of reasoning, logic

SECOND DIMENSION:
Heart = emotions, how a person feels

THIRD DIMENSION:
Soul = faith, spiritual essence of a person, keeping eternity in view

Section I also presented the various styles with which different personalities tend to approach change. What kind of changee are you? What is your normal reaction when you are confronted with a change maze? Remember that you could be any one of the following: resistor, slow follower, fast follower, or new idea person. But there are several change shapers that can move you away from the way you usually respond.

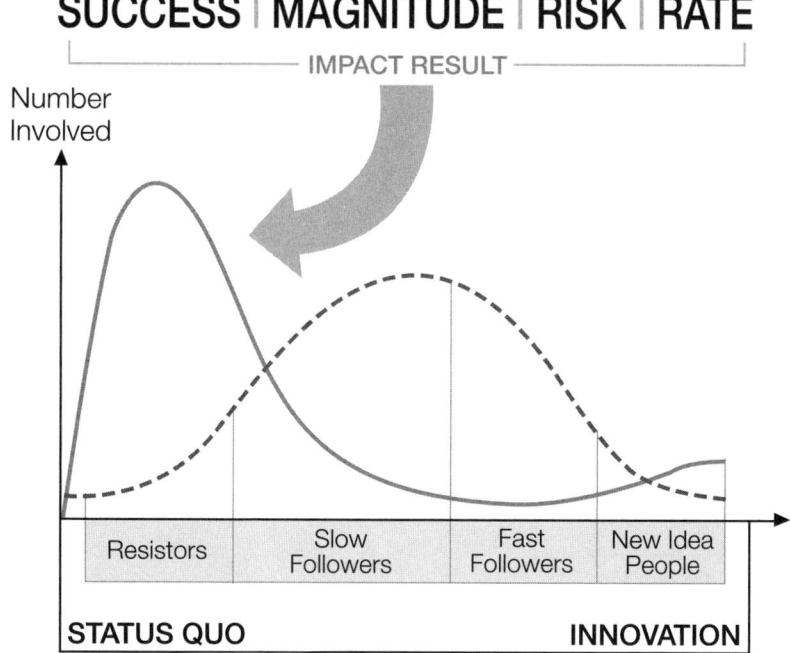

FIGURE 2.6

Change mazes that are recognizably difficult (in terms of magnitude), filled with uncertainty (in terms of risk), and have come on the scene quickly (in terms of rate) may cause you to become a resistor or slow follower.

Several fundamentals are worth remembering.

CHANGE FUNDAMENTALS

1 The rate of change in the world, generally speaking, is accelerating and becoming more sporadic (discontinuous).

2 The growing magnitude of change is amplified by increasing complexities.

3 People often apply "better sameness" in an effort to avoid required change.

4 Change abides by the law of inertia: If a body is at rest or moving at constant speed in a straight line, it will continue to do so unless it is acted upon by a force.

5 The spectrum of personalities, in terms of response to change, ranges from resistors to new idea people.

FROM SECTION 2

If you'll recall, managing yourself when you are faced with a change maze is a process and a way to think, not a formula nor a prescriptive set of rules. The first kind of change maze we considered was the predictable change, and one of the most common forms is the S-Curve of Growth.

STAGE	NAME	CHARACTERISTICS
I	Initiation	Start, beginning, new idea, conception, birth
II	Growth	Contagion, expansion, excitement
III	Control	Slower growth, more deliberation, less risk taking
IV	Maturation	Slowing down, practicality, caution, aversion to change

TABLE 3.3

But there is a back side or decay side to the S-Curve, and that side reveals two more stages. Putting all six stages together creates what is called the Life Cycle.

STAGE	NAME	CHARACTERISTICS
V	Decay	Aging, contraction, disappointment
VI	Termination	Death, closing, passing on, destruction

TABLE 4.1

Predictable changes can often provide you with a basis for planning change in order to delay, alter, or compensate for what you know is coming. For instance, as you look at the progression of career change through the past four decades, you should be able to predict the trend. This information can be used for your personal career planning, which puts you in the advantageous position of actually planning changes in your own life.

DECADE	PROGRESSION OF CAREER CHANGE
1970s	Professional climbing, or dealing with boredom, or seeking a change usually meant a change within the company
1980s	The desire to improve oneself or make a change usually caused a person to change companies
1990s	Based on the changes in the culture, marketplace, and compensation, the need for change often meant a change in careers
2000s	One major capability essential in the professional workforce is the ability to make multiple career changes throughout one's work-life

TABLE 5.1

The unpredictable change becomes more complex and difficult to navigate.

1 The change blindsides you.

2 The frequency of the change is sporadic.

3 The change hits quickly.

4 The magnitude of the change is often great.

5 Most people initially react to the change by moving to the resistance side of the Change Capacity Spectrum.

6 Changes similar to those that had yielded earlier successes may cause you to ignore or downplay the potential outcomes.

Although you may have a lot of resilience, a sporadic and blind-side change can cause you to hit the dysfunctional wall. This is a √-List to help you when you're blindsided.

BLIND-SIDE ✔LIST

✔		ACTION
	1	Get on your knees and ask God to calm you. Don't follow your emotions to run in panic.
	2	Concentrate on where you are in the labyrinth. Don't focus on how you got there.
	3	Stop and reflect. Is it the change that is causing your trauma or is it the fact that you were surprised? (When you calm down, you may see the labyrinth shrink because the change isn't such a big deal.)
	4	Look back over your experiences. Have you ever been faced with a change like this before? If so, can you remember what you did then? That experience can guide you to what you should or shouldn't do to navigate now.
	5	Call a Christ-follower friend. One you can trust to be objective and confidential. Take the time to describe the change. Ask the friend to help you distinguish between the mind and heart dimensions. Talk it through. He probably won't be able to navigate for you, but it should help clean your windshield of extraneous bugs so you can see the labyrinth corridors more clearly.
	6	Look at yourself in the Change Capacity mirror. Determine whether you've allowed the change to shove you into territory where you don't normally operate. If it has, get back to where you function the best.

How do you know if you're about to hit the dysfunctional wall? Here are some escalating signs and what your responses might be.

	SIGNS OF HITTING THE WALL	INDICATIVE RESPONSES
1	Denial	Ignore the change
2	Lack of understanding	Avoid getting the facts
3	Frustration	Plead confusion
4	Anxiety	Be upset and lose of sleep
5	Anger & Hostility	Display hostile behavior
6	Declaration that change is unacceptable	Attempt to undo the change
7	Irrational thinking (Heart takes over the Mind)	Become irrational (falsify the facts, make accusations, take steps designed to take things back to before the change, organize resistance, introduce counter-changes)
8	Sadness & self pity	Withdraw
9	Grief	Fail to function properly, remain silent or over communicate
10	Depression	Withdraw further and/or attack others
11	Unrelenting depression	Attempt suicide and/or other violent venting

TABLE 7.2

What if you catch yourself escalating through the signs (1–11 above)? A pivotal point is step 6, where you finally acknowledge that to you, the change is totally unacceptable. It is at this checkpoint that the Christ-follower can split off from the steps leading to unrelenting depression and lean on your faith in God. Replace steps 7–11 with the following:

	ACTIONS	EXPLANATION
7	Honest Prayer	Honest and fervent prayer should be a way of life for the Christ-follower, but we don't always live that way. Instead, God is brought in to help face inevitable change when we experience frustration, anxiety, and anger. Nonetheless, He listens, helps, and calms in a way that only the Christ-follower comprehends.
8	Careful Reasoning	When God is involved, He directs so that your heart and mind don't control you. He helps temper your emotions so that spirit-led thinking and careful reasoning provide support in facing change.
9	Role Reality	With steps 7 and 8 in place, you can determine whether or not there is anything you can do about the change. And if not, turn it over to the Lord and move on. If you find that you do have a role to play in the change, God will lead you to take the right actions in addressing the change.
10	Acceptance	By the time you have moved through steps 7, 8, and 9, even if the change has blind-sided you, even if it is traumatic, even if it is filled with risk, even if it is severely disliked, you can accept that the change is real and seek to learn from it and use it for eternal results.
11	Trust in God	At this stage, you recognize that God is sovereign, that His ways are beyond understanding, and that He is in control of all things. This fork-in-the-road doesn't necessarily bring good results from either the mind or the heart, but trusting in Christ brings a peace that is beyond your understanding.

TABLE 8.4

FROM SECTION 3

The discussion of the soul dimension is based on the fact that you have experienced the ultimate change; you gave your life to Jesus Christ. This change has profound results:

BEFORE CHRIST I WAS ...	AFTER CHRIST I AM ...
Dead	Alive
Lost	Found
Damned	Saved
Rejected	Accepted
Guilty	Forgiven
Hell-Bound	Heaven-Bound
Stressed	Calmed
In Conflict	At Peace
Fearful	Bold
Sad	Joyful
Self-centered	Christ-centered
Loved	Loved
Causing God Sadness	Bringing God Joy
Focused on Mind & Heart Views	Focused on Soul Views

For the Christ-follower, Christ-centeredness replaces self-centeredness. Your spiritual viewpoint puts change mazes in eternity's perspective. The facts and your emotions driven by self are pushed into the background. As the Apostle Paul wrote,

> I have been crucified with Christ; and it is no longer I who live, but Christ lives in me; and the life which I now live in the flesh I live by faith in the Son of God, who loved me and gave Himself up for me.
>
> Galatians 2:20

When you are led by God's perspective and purposes, you are equipped to deal with the difficult question, "Should I change or not change?"

CHANGE OR NOT CHANGE ✓LIST

1. Don't let your emotions get in the way of listening to the Lord.
2. Get the facts.
3. Ask friends, experts, and other Christ-followers for their counsel.
4. Ask God to lead you as you face the maze.
5. Consider what Jesus would say about you making the change.
6. Measure the change against Scripture and your spiritual belief system.
7. Remember what you have learned from similar changes already experienced in your own life.
8. Weigh the risks.
9. Estimate what the consequences might be if you change or don't change.

FIGURE 11.1

There are bedrock actions that you as a Christ-follower can take to make sound change/not change decisions.

1 Establish a way and time to walk with God each day.

2 Soak up the Scriptures.

3 Establish God-breathed core beliefs that you won't compromise.

> Therefore, if anyone is in Christ, he is a new creature; the old passed away; behold, new things have come. II Corinthians 5:17

FROM SECTION 4

What can you find out about yourself and change mazes after you've emerged from or gotten stuck in a maze? A simple review of where you fit on the Change Reaction Scale when you were first confronted with the maze compared with your place when you emerged should help prepare you to face the next change.

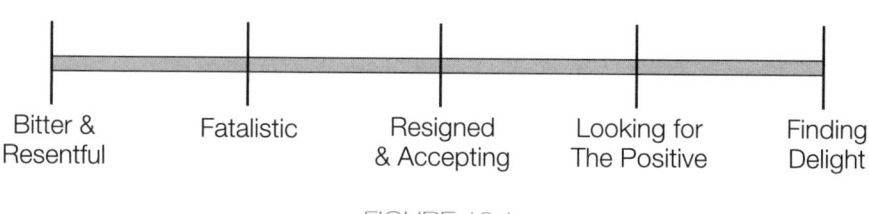

FIGURE 12.1

Christ-centered people usually move toward the right on the scale even if they initially react on the left.

> See to it that no one misses the grace of God and that no bitter root grows up and cause trouble and defile many. **Hebrews 12:15**

It is reassuring to know that God has eternal purpose in everything He does to, for, and with you. There are many absolutes that you may recognize after you've emerged from a change maze. Here are some of them.

ABSOLUTES

1. God has purpose in everything to bring Glory to Himself.

2. God loves you and takes your best interest to heart.

3. God's view of best interest is always focused on the eternal life perspective.

4. God planned and knows your future (for all eternity).

5. God sacrificed His Son, Jesus, in order to offer you a future with Him.

6. God is willing to have you sacrifice your earthly well-being to further His work.

7. God is the source of comfort and solace when the mazes overwhelm you.

8. God surrounds you with spiritual brothers and sisters to help and encourage you.

9. God builds, changes, solves, and removes change mazes in your life to get and keep you on His agenda.

10. God's plan is for you to grow to be more like Him throughout your lifetime.

TABLE 13.1

It is important—no, essential—to realize that God uses change as a key method to carry out His spiritual growth plan to make you more like Christ. As He says in Jeremiah 18:6, "Behold like the clay in a potter's hand, so are you in My hand."

FROM SECTION 5

What if you want to bring about change? You may be a new idea person who wants to be a difference maker. Or you may be called of God to lead change (even if you don't want to or don't feel adequate).

It is critical to know that the crux of leading change is that you are leading people. Here is a summary of the Marks of Leadership that will serve you well as you lead people into and through change. A successful leader does the following:

1. Respects others
2. Finds value in all people
3. Is called to lead and willing to follow
4. Is able and willing to communicate
5. Withstands pressure and stress
6. Knows when to persist and when to change
7. Is willing to stand alone
8. Takes personal risk to reduce the risk to others
9. Provides meaningful vision
10. Establishes clear direction

Selected From The Marks of Leadership[8]

[8] LGI Executive Briefing Paper

Remember, you are introducing people to change mazes that they may or may not want to enter. Depending on the change force (magnitude, type, pace), the change may drive them to take steps of resistance.

There are a few fundamental actions that can help you lead others into a change maze and at least reduce the resistance. Here is a summary.

1 Really think through the details of the change.

2 Determine the real timetable whereby the change must be accomplished.

3 Identify those people who will be impacted by the change.

4 Determine where those people are (as individuals and as a group) on the structure, culture, and life issues.

5 Build a strategy to inform and sell the concepts of the change.

6 Monitor the resistance carefully and be prepared to abandon the hard-core resistors.

7 Begin to involve the fast followers and slow followers in carrying out the change.

8 Monitor the risk of failure

9 Continue to communicate the progress of the change.

10 When the change (or a specific phase if it is a multi-phase change) is complete, celebrate the event.

11 Be sure to include the slow followers, fast followers, and converted resistors in the celebration.

12 In almost all cases, more change will be necessary because you have learned more.

Feel called to be a difference maker? Here are some questions and suggestions to help you get on the right track.

First, should you do it?

1 What is the motive for doing it?

2 Have the anticipated results of the change been carefully articulated?

3 What is the cost of doing the change?

4 Has the resistance been evaluated?

5 Is this change driven by spiritual values or ideas and emotions?

Second, how do you avoid the land mines?

1 What are your strengths related to leading the change you are called to make?

2 Build a team with the complementary skills required to make it happen.

3 Evaluate your own ability to focus, stay the course, and resolve to overcome distractions.

4 Continue to monitor the change detractors.

5 Urge every member of your team to assess whether their faith is directing their behavior and their resolve.

6 Never pass up an opportunity to communicate.

For the Christ-follower, the real peace that calms the storms of change—whether you are the changer or the changee—comes from viewing everything through the lens of eternity. The words of an old gospel song put it in perspective: "This world is not my home, I'm just a passing through." And another: "Turn your eyes upon Jesus, look full in His wonderful face. And the things of earth will grow strangely dim in the light of His glory and grace."[9]

This book couldn't come to its conclusion without one more RealityCase. It brings home the delight of shifting one's focus from the mind and heart to the soul and eternity. The ultimate change makes the Eternity View clearer as we grow to become more Christ-like.

[9] Text and music by Helen H Lemmel, Copyright 1922, Renewal 1950 by Singspiration Music

 RealityCase

World 0 - Eternity 2

These are two stories rolled into one. The first is about a man who was the image of goodness; the second is about a man who really had his life messed up. It's also about changes that came twice for each of them.

Jim Hunter had his act together. At least everyone who knew him thought so. He was a New York State Trooper with the rank of captain. Jim was big, strong, tough, tender, handsome, smart, quick, in excellent health, a dedicated family man—and above all, honest, fair, and caring. I think Jim could have run for any office in the county and everyone (except the criminals he apprehended) would have voted for him.

Don't misunderstand. Jim was no pushover. He was tough on those people and things that disrupted society: drugs, DUI, renegade truckers, illegal and immoral business practices, irresponsible driving, and family abusers. Jim Hunter was the image of morality and he lived it.

He had a delightful wife, Nancy, and two kids, Jim, Jr. and Lisa. The whole family was active in the community, and the kids were real successes in school.

But there was a major issue in Jim and Nancy's home. Nancy and the kids were actively involved at a growing church in town (they lived on a lake), but Jim said repeatedly that he didn't need that in his life. He had been taught to be a good and fine person, and the church didn't really add anything that he needed. Understand that Jim didn't mind if Nancy, Jim, Jr., and Lisa were involved, but he wasn't interested.

One Sunday during Bible Study (the class was examining the topic of Body Life about the body of believers and how they cared for one another as an honor to the Lord), Nancy broke down and explained that she was worried about Jim's relationship with Jesus Christ. He didn't have any!

Most of the class members found that hard to believe. True, he didn't show up at church except for special occasions, but he was such a positive example in the community, it was hard to imagine anyone that good who didn't walk with the Lord. As someone in class said in an effort to encourage Nancy, "Jim Hunter puts my example to shame. And I try to serve Christ every day." Well, that didn't really help Nancy. She knew where Jim stood on spiritual matters.

The class agreed on two things. One, they would pray hard for Jim to turn his heart over to Christ, and two, they'd keep Nancy's request to themselves so that Jim wouldn't think she had betrayed him by discussing such private matters with the Bible study group.

Now let's switch to the second story, about Don Preston. Don was a real success by this world's standards. But he sure didn't seem to worry about living a moral life, and he figured things were going just fine for him.

Preston had all the talents and skills that made most people envious. He was the chief information officer (CIO) for a growing high-tech company. (That means he was responsible for all of the computers and computer people in the firm.) And he was good at what he did. His bosses, his customers, the company's stockholders, and the people who worked for him thought he was great. He had a warm, rugged kind of personality. In fact he was so charming that women thought he was someone special. And although he had a beautiful wife, Joy, and two active young sons at home, he managed to move from one extramarital affair to another.

Added to his collection of talents was his musical ability. He sang a magnificent tenor and was in demand for major vocal engagements everywhere, including the concert choir when they presented *The Messiah* each year. He had played the trumpet in the U.S. Marine Band when he was 20, traveling around the world and entertaining everywhere, including the White House. Now that he was 32, he would sometimes play with bands around the state when he could get away from the office. (And that really provided him with the perfect excuse to not show up at home when he found it convenient.)

Now let's bring the two stories together. When Nancy finally asked for prayer in the Bible study class, Joy got to thinking. Yes, most people had their suspicions about Don, but no one ever talked about it. A couple of weeks later, Joy unloaded to the class about the problems in her family. No, she didn't go into details; all she said was that their marriage was about ready for a wreck and one of the reasons was her faith in Christ and Don's outright ridicule of anything to do with the Lord.

The class prayed each week when they got together. Oh, how they prayed! And class members included both Jim and Don in their personal prayer times as they got on their knees before the Lord each day.

At the same time, Mountainside Church was in the midst of a major building program. One Saturday night they held a banquet for the members and people throughout the town. It was a great occasion. The design had been completed, the permits and zoning had been approved, and there was real excitement about the future. The banquet had two purposes; one was to tell everyone about the plans and progress. The other to start the fund-raising. There was marvelous music and a guest speaker who talked about God's call for change. He only spoke for 10 minutes, but he really said a lot about God's people and their role in the future of our land.

Now Pastor Grounds was a "with it" leader. It so happens that one of the musical numbers was Don Preston playing "The Church's One Foundation" on the trumpet. Don, although he didn't come to church often, figured he'd show off his talents to a new kind of audience. And show off he did! The crowd really loved it—and let him know with long applause.

After the event was over, the pastor approached Don. "Don, would you be available to play that again tomorrow morning in church? There are lots of people who would really like to hear that again." Well, Don was turned on by the crowd's response. "Sure, Pastor, I'd be glad to do it. Just don't think that I'll show up every Sunday and get hooked by your sermons." They both laughed and then parted.

On Sunday morning, as Pastor Grounds recounted the events of Saturday night, you could tell that the Holy Spirit was in that place. He finally was so overwhelmed that he couldn't say much. All he did was ask the congregation to Give God a Standing Ovation. The place was alive for at least 10 minutes.

I don't even know what the pastor preached about that morning. But I know a couple of things. Don Preston played and the people were blessed. And Jim Hunter who had been there on Saturday night to support Nancy and participate in such an important community event also showed up that Sunday morning.

As people stood for the last hymn and closing prayer, Pastor Grounds asked everyone to pray—pray that God would continue to fill His church and His people. Lots of heads went down; this was a praying church. I remember praying for both Jim Hunter and Don Preston. As the organ played in the background and people prayed silently, I finally looked up. Lord, you didn't understand me right. The wrong Jim Hunter was on his knees at the altar. It was Jim, Jr. And then, before God and a packed house, Don Preston walked over to his wife, gave her a big hug and talked with her for a minute and then they both got on their knees.

Well, it didn't end there. Jim Hunter, Sr. joined Jim, Jr. on his knees.

The service didn't end quite on time. In fact it ran over about 45 minutes and there hadn't even been an invitation for people to get their hearts right with the Lord. But no one complained. The people had met God and God had met His people.

If one judges by their fruits, there is no doubt in my mind that Don, Jim, and Jim, Jr. truly gave their lives to Christ that day. And the actions within the next three months confirmed it.

Remember, both Jim and Don were extremely successful in their professions. In the world's eyes, they had it all, including great families, and they were super performers in their fields. And in the church's view, it was marvelous because now they were believers in Jesus

> Christ. What a right combination: believers who were also successful in the world.
>
> But God asked for more, and He got it. Within two months, Jim resigned from his position as a state trooper, gave up most of his retirement, too. Then he sold his home so that he could afford to go to seminary. He is now a pastor in North Carolina of a praying, growing, reaching, caring, Christ-honoring church.
>
> A month after Jim responded to God's call, Don resigned his executive position and sold his house in order to go to seminary. Then he and his family (the boys played trumpet, too) traveled throughout the world giving Gospel concerts. Now he is the pastor of music at a large church in the Midwest.
>
> Both of these men experienced two God-driven changes; one was to turn their lives over to the Lord. The other was the change from a secular world view of what's important about what they do for a living to the eternal view.

Change is a powerful way for God to grow His followers. He has used change mazes to break, mold, and shape me. Our Lord is intent on doing that with you, too. If you know the Potter, the chipping, spinning, rubbing, and baking can bring you joy and excitement because He is preparing to fill you with His love for His purpose and His glory.

For example, think about the change mazes of our day. Some of these may have directly impacted you or people you know.

> The translation and showing of the *Jesus* film in hundreds of countries
>
> The AIDS epidemic around the world
>
> Medical breakthroughs that make heart, kidney and joint replacements possible

The terrorist attacks in the U.S. on 9/11

Cell and satellite telephones

The tsunami catastrophe in South East Asia

Men and women leaving lucrative jobs to go into vocational Christian service

The deregulation of telephone, airline, and utility industries

Changing seasons of life

Hurricanes Katrina, Rita, and Wilma in 2005

Growing house churches in the US

The earthquake in Southern Asia

The rise in gasoline and heating prices

The homeschool movement

Moving goods in the U.S. by truck instead of trains

Illegal immigration

Computerization and automation

The use of satellites to beam the Gospel around the world

And the list goes on.

Do you have a lengthy personal list of change mazes you've been facing?

Like the previous list, some appear good and others bad; some remote and others close to home; some will pass and others will stay; some encourage us and others cause us to be almost dysfunctional. Sometimes it's difficult to grasp that God uses change to transform us to become more like Him.

In the introduction of this book, I told you that God has used change mazes to shape my life. Can you look back and see how He has confronted you with changes to shape yours?

With all the changes that God makes happen in your life, remember that "Jesus Christ is the same yesterday and today and forever." Hebrews 13:8.

The universe expands and contracts; people are conceived, live, and die; governments come and go; and through all of these changes, He is the bedrock of stability. "God is our refuge and strength, a very present help in trouble." Psalm 46:1. He is the foundation for your soul throughout all eternity.

And in conclusion—

When the trees you've hugged all your life...

come crashing down...

plant new trees!

And the peace of God which surpasses all comprehension, will guard your hearts and your minds in Christ Jesus. **Philippians 4:7**

ACKNOWLEDGEMENTS

Many individuals have been part of the positive changes that God has used to shape my life. They can't all be listed here because of space and my memory. But the following come to mind as I reflect on the inspiration for this manuscript.

Students at Baylor University—for their inquiring minds about change.

John Piper, Senior Pastor at Bethlehem Baptist—for changing my focus to desire God and increasing my longing to reflect back to Him His glory

Jimmy Long, Senior Pastor of Grace Fellowship—for his commitment to change wherever and however God leads.

Bible Study men at Reynolds Plantation—for their willingness to let me think outside the box and their love for each other and the Word.

Mercer Reynolds, CEO, and Rob Mitchell, President, of Reynolds Plantation—for their exemplary passion for positive change and relentless growth.

Participants in the *Impact: Change and the Christian* Course at First Baptist Greensboro—for their helpful ideas and patience with new material.

Christ-Followers at Grace Fellowship—for choosing to change in order to minister outside the walls.

Dan Werthman, Senior Pastor of Lakewood Church—for his commitment to leading us to an ever changing and maturing walk with our Lord no matter the cost.

Client executives—for applying the change principles in this book and then urging me to "write it down."

Tracey Finck, my editor—for her persistent penchant for focus, clarity, rewriting, rewriting, rewriting . . . until the book met her standards.

Chip Borkenhagen, owner of Evergreen Press—for getting excited about this book, using his God-given talents, and relentlessly driving to get it right.

Navigating Change Team at Evergreen: Andrea, Brad, Brian, Jodi—for their expertise, hard work, and continual encouragement.

Our children, Tom Jr., Tim (who is no longer on the human part of his spiritual journey), **Heather Jean, and their spouses, Heather Lee and Doug**—for providing countless examples of God-directed change.

Our grandkids—for providing the evidence that change is a way of life.

My mother, Reva—for a life that delights in change even now at 92.

My wife, Cheke—for being a living example of standing on the solid Rock of Jesus Christ while adapting to the changes He puts in our lives.

Jesus Christ—for providing the ultimate change in my life that made me God's child for all eternity.

FOLLOW-UP
with Tom Lutz

Lutz Group International® offers several ways for you to dig deeper into navigating change.

Navigating Change Self-Assessment*

This tool is designed to give you added insight into how you react to change and how you create change when you see it is needed. In addition to getting an analysis section to help you interpret the results, the questions and exercises will cause you to face issues about yourself that can help you build your own navigation tools.

Navigating Change Presentations*

1. Navigating Change Lecture - A presentation by Tom Lutz

2. Navigating Change Seminar – A half-day to whole-day seminar or workshop where participants get involved in presentations and exercises to examine the personal issues of change in their lives

3. Leading Change Workshop – A leadership event to help develop leadership tools that deal with both the leader's and the followers' attitudes toward and strategies for change

Navigating Change Small Group Leader's Guide

Navigating Your Change Mazes can be used as a topical book for small groups. This guide is designed to help the leader organize and facilitate the group in discovering more about themselves and how God uses change to shape their lives. (Guide*) (CD with PowerPoint Session Notes*)

Contacting Tom Lutz

To ask questions, swap ideas, place orders, or request information about LGI®, write to:

>Tom Lutz
>LGI®
>39354 S. Winding Trail
>SaddleBrooke, AZ 85739
>
>or E-Mail: Tom@LutzGroup.com

Check out our Website – LutzGroup.com

- Abstract of Book 2, *Change Tales* and projected release date

- Abstract of Book 3 addressing Change and the Church and projected release date

- Leadership help on strategies for change

- New Change Maze Navigation Tools

*Contact LGI® for prices